Back Words
My Lifelong Struggle with Dyslexia

From the darkness of illiteracy to the illumination of success:
tribulations and triumphs of a Missouri entrepreneur

by
Thomas Earl Harrawood
as told to G. L. Harrawood

Copyright © 2018 by Thomas L. Harrawood, All Rights Reserved

Back Words. No part of this publication may be reproduced, distributed, or transmitted in any form or by any means, including photocopying, recording, or other electronic or mechanical methods, without the prior written permission of the author, except in the case of brief quotations embodied in critical reviews and certain other noncommercial uses permitted by copyright law. For permission requests, email the publisher, with the subject line "Attention: Permissions Coordinator," at the email address below.

Although every precaution has been taken to verify the accuracy of the information contained herein, the Author and Publisher assume no responsibilities for errors or omissions. No liability is assumed for damages that may result from the use of information contained herein.

Printed in the United States of America

First Printing, 2017

Books may be purchased in quantity by contacting the publisher directly at stellarpub@gmail.com or at the website www.stlrpress.com.

ISBN (print, hard cover):978-1-932860-09-2
ISBN (print, soft cover): 978-1-932860-07-8
ISBN (ebook): 978-1-932860-08-5

Biography

Stellar Press
email: stellarpub@gmail.com

Dyslexia: a general term for disorders that involve difficulty in learning to read or interpret words, letters, and other symbols, but that do not affect general intelligence.

- The New Oxford American Dictionary

Persistence: firm or obstinate continuance in a course of action in spite of difficulty or opposition.

- The New Oxford American Dictionary

Back Words

Table of Contents

	Foreword	1
	Introduction	3
1	Bloodlines	5
2	Harris House	23
3	A Scholar	43
4	The Smith House	63
5	Hoosier Land	81
6	The Basement House	95
7	Last Days of Hoosier School	127
8	Departure	139
9	Seventy-two	149
10	A Darn Fool	171
11	Snow and Men	187
12	"Play Ball"	205
13	From Out of the Ashes	215
	Epilogue	227
	Photographs	115

Foreword

At the moment of conception two halves of chromosomes unite to make one particularly unique individual. Millions of genes merge to create every aspect of what that person is to become. From the color of ones eyes to the probability of disease propensities, the die is cast for a lifetime. What one does with that potential is the ultimate question. Why or how the merging of one specific genetic group creates the ability or inability to discern words or their meaning or the ability to understand, remember or contemplate their combinations is an underlying premise throughout this book. For reasons yet unknown, Tom had and has a condition most of you readers cannot either understand or contemplate the difficulties it creates. It helped to define him early to his friends, his family and to himself. It created barriers throughout his life that have at times held him back, caused him self doubt, but mostly challenged him to overcome. As you will see, in most cases forced him to develop unique skills to compensate for and defeat its consequences.

Tom Harrawood is as unique a personality as anyone could ever meet. How this particular aspect of his life helped or hindered his potential is up for discussion; let the professionals consider that. What cannot be disputed, however, is that Tom took this challenge head on, made no excuses, accepted the facts and molded his life in spite of its limitations. Anyone experiencing the same condition can take heart in the fact that nothing can or should hold you back but yourself. Learn from people like

Back Words

Tom. Learn that there is always more than one way to solve a problem or to be successful. Learn that you define you!

~ Mike Kohnen, a friend

Introduction

Just as I have for many Missouri mornings, I stand at the gas range, striking a match to the rising gas of an even blue flame as I set my tea kettle to boil water for my morning Lipton. I look out the kitchen window over my Franklin County farm and scan the barns, sheds, and stock pens where Laura, my wife, raises her llamas and milk cow. In a glance I recognize the perimeter as "ship shape" with the detailed eye of an old Navy Bo'sun Mate who catches anything not in order.

My constitution in life is to be an organized man, and this is one of the many reasons I have succeeded in life's endeavors. But this morning the tea has become my saliva, and breakfast will be a very bland concoction of paste-like oatmeal that none of my taste buds will recognize. They know nothing of the past, for they have been burned by thirty-two radiation treatments (in about as many days) for throat cancer—a cancer that was discovered while I was being treated for lymphoma and also recovering from open heart surgery. But heck, I've had a broken back from working draft horses, broken noses from bucking cows, and gotten into fistfights with Sailors, Marines, and even my own dear Dad, who we called Frank. I have always healed, made amends, and prepared for whatever nature, God, or my own stupidity would deal out next.

However, the greatest of all my challenges was a learning disability: primarily, the inability to read or write, and the long struggle of being thought of as the dumb kid in the class. Second grade was the toughest, and it was in the second grade that I would remain not once, but two times. If it wasn't for teachers being good neighbors, I would still be there in Miss Hunter's second grade class. The fact is I never officially got promoted further than the third grade. Instead, I was simply passed to the next grade, and the next, all the way through high school, where I stayed only until I could legally quit.

Yet I have come to judge myself a successful business man. This is the story of my long struggle with the disorder, unknown in my early life, of dyslexia. This is also the story of how I learned my way amid the ribbing, embarrassment, and absolute terror of being discovered that I could not read. I could not see the picture painted by words. This is not an appeal for pity, nor have I ever sought it out. This is a story of a ferociously proud American patriot, raised in a Post-World War II Indiana, who took the tools that nature gave and used the freedom provided by the sacrifices of others to stand here this Missouri morning and reminisce. This is also the account of how the textures of clay and the hues of colors that the Master Potter used to knead, mold, and fire my life's experiences, failures, and successes, have developed this human vessel known as Thomas Earl.

CHAPTER ONE

Bloodlines

My great grandfather, Abner Francis, was born in 1875, and his wife, Lulu Harrawood, was born in 1881. Abner was a bull of a man, with hunching shoulders and huge warts on his face. His lips were thick and twisted to the corner of his mouth from chewing tobacco, giving him a well-stained brown crevasse running from the corner of his mouth and down his chin. I cannot say with certainty that Lulu chewed, but she looked a lot like her husband, warts and all. Some of their looks passed on to their son, my grandpa, William Arnold Harrawood, born January 1897, but thankfully this strain of genes washed out by the time it got to me.

The Harrawood family met up with the John Gregory family somewhere down in the Texarkana country, and traveling with John was their daughter Elsie Valentine Gregory, born February 14, 1898. Why the Harrawoods were in this part of the country is lost in history. The John Gregory family, however, was bringing up a string of horses. This is where my grandparents met, and as the two families worked themselves up through Arkansas and finally to Illinois, Elsie Valentine Gregory was "showing." William Arnold Harrawood and Elsie Valentine Gregory were united in holy matrimony and thus the origin of my father, Francis Earl Harrawood, born February 28, 1916. My father's name was derived from my great grandfather, Abner Francis, and another of his sons, my great uncle Earl Harrawood.

Back Words

My grandmother Elsie and her new husband, William Arnold, set up home in Eldorado, Illinois, the southeast part of the state. The North Fork of the Saline River cuts through Saline County, crosses the top of Eldorado, then skirts to the south down on the east side and eventually dumping into the Ohio River. Directly east of Eldorado, the Wabash River merges with the Ohio River that established the eastern border of Illinois. This delta made for good farming when it wasn't flooded. While Oklahoma was experiencing a dust bowl, Eldorado farm lands were often a muddy soup bowl, which just added more burden and drudgery during the Great Depression.

The Gregorys continued their caravan and worked themselves on over to southern Indiana. Now, it is widely known, or at least traceable anyhow, that a certain measure of insanity came from Grandma's side of the family. Well, that's Grandpa's argument anyway. Some say it's because Cherokee blood may have mixed with the Gregory's blood, giving the Harrawoods their insane temperament. Personally, I don't blame the Indians.

There is a little bit of fog in the history of why my grandparents moved to Indiana, since William Arnold had no family there. I think Grandma Elsie just wanted to get away from the Harrawoods and take her clutch to be near her Gregory family. Or, it could be that because the Gregorys were nomadic like Gypsies, Grandma Elsie just wanted to roam again. Whatever the reason, Grandpa Arnold and Grandma Elsie eventually migrated to the same southern Indiana lands. Elsie bore another son, Leo, a daughter, Gladys, another son Paul, plus three more: Ollie Everett, Nellie, and Laura Rose.

My mother, Vivian Ellen Moorehead, came into the world on March 7, 1920, and was raised in the same Eldorado locale as my father.

Chapter 1 - Bloodlines

Vivian's father worked deep in the mines much like other Saline County men, until one day a slab of the mine ceiling dropped and killed him.

Another horrendous mishap struck Vivian's family during an afternoon social gathering. Vivian's mother was hosting lunch at her house for the local ladies. After they had eaten, they gathered in another room, leaving everything out, including some lye, which one of the ladies wanted to borrow. It was sitting alongside the ice tea. When Vivian's brother came in from the mines and saw the tea, he decided to pour all the containers into one, including the one with lye, which he probably assumed was sugar. He poured himself a glass, put the glass to his lips and, tipping his head back, swallowed his death. He burned from the inside out. The only relief, if it was that at all, was that he was taken to the showers at the mines in an effort to keep him comfortable until he died.

Mom had two sisters (as far as I know). One of them, Aunt Lois, was married to Thomas Earl McKinley, who was my namesake, Thomas Earl. Aunt Lois was one of Mom's sisters and the one I knew best. Her other sister, Lilly, migrated down into Kentucky, and her sister Ellen died when I was a young child. She also had two brothers, Arthur, who was twenty years her senior, and Fred, also her senior.

Uncle Fred was a career Navy man who served during the Great War to end all wars. He was out on the West Coast and, for reasons lost, he was forcefully, but with honor, discharged from the Navy. He moved out to Pasadena, California, which would give impetus in later years to a great family adventure.

My father, who we all called Frank, remained in Eldorado after Grandpa and Grandma migrated to Indiana. My mother was just sixteen when she married Frank in 1936. I only have bits and pieces of their time in the Land of Lincoln, and, I suppose, like everyone else in those gun-slinging days of Pretty Boy Floyd and the G-Men, they were just trying to live as honest as most everyone else. After all, Frank had great Harrawood characteristics: he was big, strong, and not afraid to fight or work hard. So when the opportunity for this handsome dark-eyed man with bushy eyebrows (that could be menacing when provoked) to become deputy sheriff presented itself, Frank jumped at it. A deputy in the rambling, but roaring historic Shawneetown, on the Ohio River near the Saline Mines in Gallatin County, would certainly require someone without shaky knees. Frank was the man.

Shawneetown had the well-earned reputation of being on the seedy side of civilization. It was rife with bootleggers and gangsters. Heck yes! This was Illinois during the "Dirty Thirties" wasn't it? How long Frank was a deputy, I don't know, but his lawman days ended the very day gangsters tied the sheriff to the running board of a Ford, which then sped off out of town. The sheriff was found shot clean through his heart, leaving him to bleed to death on river road dust, according to Frank.

Just as well for Frank, since things were heating up big time over in Europe. This Adolph Hitler guy was building a big fire, and America began feeling the heat. No matter that Americans just really didn't see it as their fight. The Nazis had created the conflagration, which became World War II.

Mr. Franklin Delano Roosevelt won his reelection in a landslide, and between FDR and Hitler, the Depression unofficially came to a close. Frank and Vivian packed up whatever they had to call theirs and headed to Detroit, Michigan, via a short passage through Indiana.

By 1938 Frank and Vivian were living in Detroit, where they had their first two boys: Gayle in 1938, followed by Edward Arnold in 1940. The babies came quickly, and it was said that they were born nine month and fifteen minutes apart. The Eldorado migrants passed through Indiana and stayed at my grandparent's for a short time. Frank would have been reacquainted with his brothers and sisters, and they with Vivian. A picture of the family shows Frank, gingerly and very tenderly, holding his sister, little Nellie. Little Nellie was born on September 6, 1930, and in one photograph I have of her as a young girl, she looks to be about eight years old. The only one who is missing in the photograph is Leo, who lived in greater Detroit at that time.

Frank and Vivian settled in Detroit, where he took employment as a bus driver and mechanic for the Martin Bus Line. Leo had earlier planted his feet there too. Having a family and economic considerations were the catalysts that likely sent my parents there.

The Michiganders may have more than once traveled back south to Indiana to visit family in the three and a half to four years they lived in Detroit. One thing is certain, they were in Indiana on August 29, 1941. That is when Nellie was laid to rest at the Bethany graveyard after whooping cough stole her life. This is about all I can remember being told of this time. Perhaps it was after December 7 of the same year that provoked Mom and Frank, with their two boys and Tommy "in the hopper," to move to Alfordsville, Indiana in 1942.

It would be a short stay at Alfordsville, taking just enough time for me to be born at home. At birth, my Father said, "I was so ugly, he took me out to a tree to see if I barked or cried!"

That tree was more likely dying or dead, on an old dilapidated farmstead, in the county of Daviess, the township of Reeve, near the village of Alfordsville, Indiana.

Alfordsville was established by James Alford in the 1830s and was an island of a village, where its geographic location made it a place few would pass through and even fewer would stay, other than those who would call it home. There was no planned Erie-Wabash canal to go through or near. When the railways began it was the same. The town's only purpose was a place for surrounding folks to go to church, buy groceries, and get buried.

The heart of the town still had a pulse in 1942, but the Great Depression had sucked out most of the life from its commerce and its people. Just like the erosion of the land, folks and small homesteads were already melting away in search of a better life. This latter fact was a benefit to our family as it gave us vacant places to rent, and, as I shall later describe, where we found the deserted homes that the Harrawoods and the groundhogs fought over.

When I came into this world it was the month of blooming peonies, May 21, 1942. I must have come through that part okay, other than howling at the tree, since there were no other complications noted concerning my birth. Decoration Day (later named Memorial Day) observance would come in a couple of weekends, and as an infant I cannot say if I had attended this solemn rite. Perhaps I did, but in 1942 fresh sod was being churned up in many graveyards across the nation, and Decoration Day began to take a greater significance for Americans everywhere for good reason: four hundred thousand Americans had landed in North Africa; Japan had taken Bataan and the Bataan Death March had begun; Nazi gas chambers and ovens had fired up; the Battle of the Coral Sea had been fought and won by our Navy; Doolittle had bombed Tokyo; and Mr. Roosevelt's government had moved a hundred thousand Japanese-Americans (called Nisei) inland from the West Coast. Surely what must have been unsettling for our Alfordsville neighbors, however, was that Mr. Hoover's G-Men had captured German saboteurs on the East Coast.

A world war had ratcheted up great changes in the summer months of '42 to meet production required for victory in Europe. The rationing of gasoline, sugar, and tires for cars was about to begin, while manufacturing of cars would stop altogether. All of this created great changes in our family, as it had for all Americans. Frank sensed that he would be called up to serve in the defense of the nation. While he still had time before gas rationing began, he loaded up and hauled his family north to Detroit, Michigan. Frank reckoned he could work at war production and his family would be near other family folks if and when he did go off to war. It was a return trip for my older brothers Gayle, now four, and Edward Arnold two. Because of this turbulent time and turn of events, I was the only one born in Indiana—a native "Hoosier." The world at war would not circumvent the Harrawood family.

"My Country Needed Me"

Frank Knox, the Secretary of the Navy, on December 4, 1941, boldly stated, "No matter what happens, the U.S. Navy is not going to be caught napping. …" Three days later on December 7 at Pearl Harbor, napping is exactly what the Navy was doing. The surprise Japanese attack at 7:55 a.m. that Sunday morning didn't just wake the Navy at Hawaii but a whole nation came out of its isolationist slumber. For the 2,403 who died as a result of the Japanese attack, an eternity of sleep was their fate. Before it was all settled, many more Americans would find everlasting sleep.

FDR, addressing Congress, called it a day that would "live in infamy." For the rest of America, however, remembering Pearl Harbor, became the WWII rallying cry. The martial arms of history hugged Frank and guided him, along with his brothers, into this conflict.

My Uncle Leo Edward Harrawood's records indicate that he was inducted into the service on December 31, 1943. Through 1944 Leo had fought in European and African campaigns, acquiring a Bronze Star for his efforts. Somewhere in the French Campaign, on October 9, he was wounded and earned a Purple Heart. He would, once again, be seriously wounded in France on November 9 and awarded the Oak Leaf Cluster with his Purple Heart. Shortly thereafter, Leo was shipped to Billings General Hospital, Fort Benjamin Harrison in Indiana, where he was given an Honorable Discharge. He then went home to a Battle Creek, Michigan hospital to recuperate from his wounds and receive total disability. Leo never fully healed from his wounds but went on to raise a family and become a successful businessman.

For William Arnold and Elsie's next son, Paul Ernest Harrawood, his recorded entry into the Army was October 1942. A photo of Paul and twenty-three more enlistees shows him squatting far right of the center rank of men. He is the only one who has a wonderful full smile, almost a laugh. The others in the photo just barely break a smile. I was born five months before that photo was taken. I would like to think that Uncle Paul had been introduced to me before he left for Europe.

Sgt. Paul was in the 330th Infantry, Eighty-third Infantry Division. The Eighty-third Infantry was activated on August 15, 1942, and was reorganized at Camp Atterbury, Indiana, about eighty miles northeast of William Arnold and Elsie's homestead. Uncle Paul would have been near his home until April 6, 1944, when his division shipped out across the Atlantic, arriving in England on April 16. He sent an Easter card to his mother that was dated April 9, 1944, from his ship on the way to England, or as soon as he got to England. Paul signed, "From your Son Paul, I'll be seeing you when this is all over hope that's soon."

Paul and his unit then landed at Normandy on June 18, 1944, at Omaha beach, twelve days after D-Day. The Division was slammed into the "battle of the hedgerows," fighting south of Carentin and reaching St. Lo-Peries road in July. From there the Eighty-third Infantry fought August through September at Dinard, St. Malo, St. Servan, and along the

Chapter 1 - Bloodlines

Loire River.

Paul's next engagement would be the Hurtgen Forest, an area of "interlocked bald, exposed ridge lines and deeply wooden ravines" with the Roer river cutting through the middle of the forest and out across the Rhine plain. On December 3, 1944, his regiment moved into this dark and bloody ground. It was here that Uncle Paul was killed that day from Nazi shrapnel. He was interred in plot MMM, row 6, Grave 119, at the U.S. Military Cemetery eighteen miles northeast of Liege, Belgium.

Hurtgen Forest is considered the worst defeat suffered by the U.S. Army. During those three months of combat, the GIs sustained nearly 33,000 casualties, and military historians would say accomplished almost nothing. In that action, in the European Theater, the Harrawood boys paid the price.

My grandparents received their first official notice in early January 1945. It reported that Paul was missing in action. They also received official notice that Leo was gravely wounded and would probably never walk again. But the telegram they received in late January stabbed them through their hearts. It confirmed that Paul was dead.

My Uncle Ollie Everett Harrawood would soon be participating in the Pacific Theater. Everett, Grandma Elsie's youngest son, entered U.S. Navy service May 30, 1944. He volunteered for the Naval Combat Demolition Units (NCDU), but immediately after he received this training he volunteered for a special unit, forming at Fort Pierce, Florida. It combined the Marine Scout and Raider's philosophy and cross-training for Naval Combat Demolition skills, and required weeks of intensive training. Uncle Everett was a member of the eighth class that graduated. This class made up the bulk of the twelfth team that was commissioned as Underwater Demolition Team 12 (UDT 12).

There is no surviving letter from or to Everett on the news about

Paul's death or Leo's grave wounds. At the time of Paul's demise, the Navy gave notice that Everett was on a submarine and his location was unknown. This was a cover, for at the very time of Paul's death, Everett and his team were in Maui preparing for the Iwo Jima invasion. The team would receive the first Presidential Unit Citation for their courage at Iwo Jima. Uncle Everett was also awarded a Bronze Star with the V device, for valor.

During this time, Mom may have been humming to the popular tunes of the day, such as "I Left My Heart at the Stage Door Canteen" or "That Old Black Magic" whereas Gayle and Ed might have been singing "Praise The Lord and Pass the Ammunition." Me? I would have been tucked in a bundle of blankets and held by Mom on our way back to Detroit in 1942.

The earliest memory I have was sitting behind the steering wheel while Frank was driving, swaying from left to right; a high-water mark and the earliest recollection I have as a baby. To substantiate anything of my infant years I'll turn to the written words from my parents' surviving letters.

Our address was 37 W. Mahon, Hazel Park, Michigan. Frank and Vivian were working to refurbish their home. They were scraping off wallpaper and sanding down woodwork.

By July 24, 1944, Mom had all four of her boys, including James Harrawood, the baby. "Jimmie," she writes to Grandma Elsie "is in his jumper seat and watches the others swing." Mom spent her time canning and gardening, and she often got mad at me for messing up my pants. "I never seen such a kid, he yells [and] cries all the time."

Frank worked the night shift as a mechanic and a bus driver for Martin Bus Lines. At this time, he was still deferred from military duty.

Mom would wake him at supper time. It was one of these evenings when he was waking up that he heard Mom when she screamed out "Shut up or I'll kill every one of you." She was frustrated from me crying, Ed "whining for his spoon" and Gayle who was "talking his head off about something." This rant of hers did not sit well with Frank. She and Frank "fussed awhile for the first time in ages." He called her up later from work to apologize, but let her know "it's not good to say things like that to the kids." Mom replied that "they had just about drove me crazy." She wrote that Frank said "yes, he had notice that," and Mom started fussing again with him.

She was also five months pregnant with Lois Ann. She wrote that she was glad Elsie was coming up while she was having the baby. Getting Frank ready for his night shift and trying to "refurbish" the house during the day, working in her garden, and taking care of the kids was a frustrating job, and Mom let anyone know who cared to listen.

Frank was inducted into the Army, on February 27, 1945, but he "went down… and enlisted" [sic] into the Navy Construction Battalion (CB). "Seabees" paid more than the Army and this would help Mom. His civilian experience qualified him for a non-commissioned position of Petty Officer Second Class (PO2). He wrote Elsie that he was going to train as a Crane or a Patrol Grader operator.

Mom wrote Elsie on March 4 that Frank went in for his physical and she "hoped he wouldn't pass (My Birthday Present)."

Frank was on his way to the war and put $125 into the car, including new tires. She was in turmoil, deciding whether she should stay in Michigan or go to Eldorado or Cannelburg, Indiana, where my grandparents lived. Mom found time to write Elsie about me. "Remember how Tommy used to call everyone a Brat when he got mad at them now he call's [sic] them asshole. He doubles up his fist and says, 'me put you in Hospital.' Boy is he mean."

Frank was now in Navy training in Rhode Island. On April 24 he was at Davisville, Rhode Island Naval Recruit Training Center. In correspondence to Elsie he was concerned with where Mom should stay, whether with Elsie, Mom's Mom in Eldorado, or there in Michigan. Only five days later he wrote to share Elsie's commiseration of Paul's death. "Well Mom I was sorry to hear about Paul." The history is lost as to when he became aware, but I can only imagine how he must have felt. In a letter in May he wrote that he was "awful lonesome tonight I wish I was out of this…place."

With Frank in the Navy, Mom was now alone and holding it all together the best she could. Her hands were full with Jimmie, who nearly died from meningitis and required medicine, and the boys, who were often a nuisance. She wrote, "that she just wasn't sure how to be fair when it came to punishment" of them.

Mom and Elsie were collaborating with Frank to get him out on a possible hardship discharge, probably based on Paul's death. He wrote, "Mother I hope you can do something about getting me out of here as I would like to be home with Vivian and the kids." In this same June 7 letter, Frank mentioned Everett. "I hope Everett gets to come back to the states for he has seen enough of that hell over there."

If being lonely, worried about his brother Everett, and being heartsick about Paul's death was not enough on Frank's plate, he wrote his mother that he received a letter from Mom that "Jimmie is so sick that doctors hold out no hope for him to live." Frank then suggests that he will be shipping out to California soon.

About this same time, Mom's mother in Eldorado suddenly died. Mom loaded us up and we headed down there and stayed for some time. While she was lonely with her mother and Frank gone, she wrote that the kids were enjoying themselves with visits to her sister in Providence,

Kentucky, her relatives in Evansville, and my grandparents' home at Cannelburg. I believe Mom needed the company more than anything during those uncertain times. We might have been something of a boll weevil family, bouncing around in four states and sleeping on the floors, but we were getting by.

Meanwhile, Frank was becoming increasingly frustrated with his plight. He wrote: "[I'll] be so … lazy…they will finally throw [me] out… [it's] going to take 4 officers to keep me at it until they either throw me out or give me something to do that amounts to something and helps get the war over." He believed it was only a matter of time before he would be heading West. The last surviving letter is dated June 28, 1945. He wrote that he would be leaving on July 7th or 9th, and he enclosed his new address as Replacement Group, N.C.T.C. (Navy Construction Training Command).

On July 16, Mom wrote to Elsie that she was waiting on a phone call from Frank to tell her goodbye before he goes overseas.

There is a photo of Frank and Uncle Everett in uniform. It was taken in a photographer's studio. Everett is standing to the right of Frank in front of a façade of palms and subtropical flora. Both are in full dress Navy blues; neither one has any military ribbons on his uniform. Everett has what may be a name tag on his right side. Frank is decorated with rings on both ring fingers, a wrist watch on his right arm, and with some sort of bracelet on his left. Both of their white "Dixie" caps are tilted back and the waves of their hair show. The grinning of both men is at full beam. Both have deep dimples at each corner of their broad grin, and both have jutting jaws. Frank had a darker complexion and his black hair only accented his furrowed dark eyebrows. The Petty Officer "crow" can be seen on each of their uniforms, and both had the same naval designation of a ships propeller, recognizing them as Motor Machinist Mates. Above Frank's crow is the famous Seabee patch of a bee holding tools and a machine gun. On the back is an inscription in Everett's handwriting that reads, "Your Two Navy Blue Sons Francis and Everett." It is the only photo I know where Elsie's Navy Sailors stood together. There is no date, and it is after Everett returned from the Pacific theater of war. Frank would not be going overseas, which may explain the explosive grin of both brothers. WWII had come to its end.

Back in Detroit, Frank came home, took off his Navy uniform, and changed into another kind of outfit. Mom and all us kids were in Detroit waiting for a bus. When it pulled up and its door opened, who but Frank was the operator. I tell you how impressed I was of Frank in his uniform, with that hat tilted back and slightly to the side providing the appearance of confidence. I might also say I was just as impressed that Mom ushered us through the turnstile while not dropping any coins or tokens into the box, even though Frank was a master at giving change with his high-speed McGill change maker on his belt. For as long as Frank drove, we rode, on his routes anyway, free.

But the war was not over for Grandma Elsie. There were several correspondences with the war department about Paul's entombment. Her persistance lasted into mid-February 1947, when she was finally notified by Major James L. Prenn, of the Quartermaster General Memorial Division. He informed her of the whereabouts of Paul's remains, at Liege, Belgium, and what she had to do to retrieve him. With some help from the Red Cross, Elsie cut through red tape bureaucracy. Finally, Paul was on his way home to be interned at Bethany Christian Cemetery.

I remember being there and that brisk cold wind whipping across the grave stones on December 19, 1947. It was two o'clock in the afternoon and how vividly I remember that it was a gray and cold December day. I remember that Everett and Leo, along with Frank, refused to let Grandma Elsie open Paul's casket. She wanted to make sure her son Paul was home. Grandma had a right to know that Paul was indeed home.

I remember Uncle Leo with his rubber contraction bands down over his shoulder and stretched to his legs, which enabled him to walk. I remember the anguished cries of Grandma, and I remember most of all the deep solemn respect from Frank, Uncle Everett, and Uncle Leo. I remember there on his fresh engraved stone the inscription, "My Country Needed Me."

Mikey the Monkey Story

I can vividly call to mind the memory of a most spectacular sport that my brothers and a new found friend, Joey, played shortly after this solemn time. We called it "Race the Monkey."

Our neighbors in a back alley yard kept a monkey that was tethered to a post. The post was six feet high, and Mikey would perch on top, well away from stray dogs or any other threat. When our gang would meander over, it was for a manly purpose—to test the monkey. Mikey would acknowledge us with growl when he saw us coming near his perimeter. But we boys knew his limits, because he was on a ten-foot lead. A definitive line existed where his reach ended. Our goal was to have one boy after another test the animal's speed.

"Cheat…cheat…err…cheat!" Mikey would say to us, flashing his teeth and making a high-pitched sound. He clutched the top of the pole and, hunching down, would make a sudden lurch toward us.

That was the game signal for a player to step up. The object was to see who could get closest to the pole before the monkey, half jumping and half scrambling down the pole, gave chase to a player. The player would run as fast as he could to the goal line with Mikey right behind. The real point of the game was to see who the monkey could catch. The belly laughs still hurt me today when I recall how he nearly ran up the rear end of one of us. Mikey would skedaddle back up the pole, and someone would yell, "Next player!"

This game went on for a few days. No one ever noticed that the length of the lead could be adjusted, and we never considered that Mikey's owner could change the rules of the game. But like all games, sometimes the other side takes the trophy. This particular day belonged to Mikey.

Joey was something of a gangly kid with bushy hair and who was just a tad slow. It was his turn to be the first player this fine summer day. He stepped up and with the rest of us behind him in a semicircle, he commenced to harass the monkey. Here's what happened:

Joey took a step toward his opponent.

Mikey just sat there on his pole.

Joey waved his arms and called out to get Mikey's attention.

But Mikey just sat there on his pole.

Joey made a little sideways hop forward.

Nothing.

Then Joey got brave and ran toward the pole. That's when Mikey came flying off the top of that pole. Joey kicked up alley gravel like a hell hound, and just when it seemed he was going to make it, we discovered that Mikey was given just enough new lead to catch Joey by the leg.

Now over the years I've heard some horrible screams, but the one I heard that day was epic. That monkey wrapped his legs and arms around Joey's leg and started chewing up his pants leg like he hadn't had a bite of food for a week. We learned our lesson that day: never take anything for granted and respect your opponents. Mikey won the trophy that day, which was half of Joey's overalls. Game over.

Our life on Mahon Street was over too. By late winter of 1948, whatever may have influenced Frank to do so, I don't know, but we packed up and left Detroit. Our family was moving back to Indiana.

Back Words

CHAPTER TWO

Harris House

The Harrawood family was now absolute and consisted (in birth order) of Gayle, Ed, Me, Jim, and Lois, with new adventures ahead for us. Frank had acquired a home just south of U.S. Route 50, on the Old Fox Road just a little way outside of Cannelburg, Indiana. Sometime during the late spring, we moved in to what was to be known in family lore as the Harris House. You may recall earlier that I alluded to the fact that Frank always found houses that were occupied by groundhogs, mice, rats, snakes, sparrows, or skunks.

This was post-war Indiana 1948, and on Frank's behalf, these homes may have been the only ones available to us. The baby boom was really just beginning to explode, and this part of Indiana was still recuperating from the Great Depression. Nevertheless, they sheltered us reasonably, and this particular house would be home sweet home for four years.

Usually the homes we lived in had windows that were cracked or shattered, and if there were screens over the windows you can bet they were sun-rotted, or curled back full of paper wasp nests and mud daubers. There is no other smell like the smell of a home that had been deserted for a long time. The scene was usually the same: tin can lids tacked over mouse holes, curled and faded wallpaper, or not even wallpaper at all, but old newspaper pasted up as a substitute. On the kitchen wall, a calendar was often left hanging, giving hint to the last time the place was lived in. Dry and dusty to the nose, a whiff of mouse poop always permeated the air, with various papers and old magazines littering the floor. Most often a stained chamber pot with the mummified remains of a mouse in it was a parting gift left behind by former occupants, which we reused. When you have nothing, everything becomes something of worth.

Where cooking or heating stoves once stood, there were open pipes, with creosote-stained rivulets running down the wall.

While Mom would go through any cabinets, if she was so lucky to have some, we kids would peep through every room and closet, and check out the view from every window of rooms upstairs that were pretty much all alike. It was upstairs in this particular house on Old Fox Road that we boys would, for four winters, keep from freezing at night by placing horse blankets, with the buckles still attached, over the top of us. Frank, Mom, and baby Lois slept downstairs.

After thoroughly investigating the inside of the homes we lived in, we boys would next move to the out buildings. If we saw the well pump it would be one of the first utilities that we tried out, and, with luck, it brought forth water without being primed. Up next to the Harris House and right outside the kitchen was a cistern with a pitcher pump. This was the water supply, and we carried water into the house in a chipped up white-enameled water bucket, with dings all about it. It was probably a used bucket when we got it. We used a long dipper with a red handle to get the water out.

One day, my Uncle Everett was helping Frank clean out the cistern when his pant leg was caught by the starter pulley of the water pump that was "borrowed" from the coal mine. It created severe lacerations and bruises, but, thankfully, there were no broken bones. It stirred quite a bit of commotion, as I remember, and also some new words for my future vocabulary.

In our homes, there was no indoor plumbing, and it was one of my jobs while there in the Harris House to take the chamber pots and empty them out in the privy. Our outhouse was a new two-hole that Frank made from rough cut lumber he got from a local sawmill. It was very proud construction that he doted on a lot. I don't remember any one digging a hole, so it must have been built and placed over the old hole.

We did have electrical power but it wasn't all that reliable, and the only outlet was the wire hanging down from the center of the ceiling. A Bakelite socket attached to the wiring allowed a light bulb to be screwed in with a chain-pull to activate the light and a plug-in for an extension. This was the way the rural electrification took place during the late thirties. I remember being told the story of a farmer on down south of us. When the rural electrification men brought power into the house, they informed the farmer that they would be back the next day to finish things up and bring with them a light bulb. That night the old farmer stuffed a rag in the socket so as not to let the "juice" flow out during the night. That's how new electricity was in this area.

When we had finally all settled in at Harris House, Mom cooked on a coal oil stove, and we made sufficient use of coal oil lamps. After all these years, I can still smell burning coal oil knotted with the aroma of dumplings and red beans. For heat we had a couple of potbelly stoves that we fueled with coal. Those of us who were raised with this type of heat will never forget waking up in the morning and hacking up coal dust "lungers." Who could forget the sulfur clouds that lingered over the house on cold winter mornings?

Frank, when he wasn't at the American Legion hall or a local bar, worked as a mechanic. When autumn came coal mining picked up and Frank could reliably find employment. This provided us with the heating fuel we used; certainly one of the perks was free coal, especially if you worked nightshift. The slope and shaft mines of yesterday were closed down with nothing but old shaft entrances and coal shakers standing as a reminder.

One day coal was being hauled from a mine south of us where Frank was working. The truck driver was coming up over the hill when our little calf spurted across the road. It was hit by the coal truck, killing it. The driver and I tossed a rope over a limb and hoisted the calf up. I ran to get a wash tub, and the driver slit the calf's throat, which bled out into the tub. Later, Frank came and we butchered that little feller up. It was heck to pay that night for letting the calf out, though there wasn't a fence hardly standing to begin with. The calf was our "fat'n up" calf from our Jersey milk cow. We always kept a fresh milk cow so as to have a good supply of milk. It was also about that time that I started learning how to milk a cow, which was one of my chores.

Another chore at this time was feeding the chickens. One morning, while "fling'n" them some hand-shelled corn, a big red-tailed hawk came swooping down on one of the hens, barely five feet in front of me, terrifying me so bad; I ran as hard as I could back to the house.

Once we got situated in our house, we scrambled to create a garden. We borrowed "Old John" the mule from our neighbor, the Williams', to plow up our garden. He was led down to our house by Uncle Everett, as we all went in for dinner. Everett hitched the mule to the front bumper of a Model A Ford, parked out in the drive. We were all sitting down at the table, when we heard a commotion outside of the window. We could see the long ears of that mule going by, and everyone 'beat feet' to get outside only to see Old John pulling the Ford down the sloping drive way. The car was picking up speed. Old John was trying to turn and run with the runaway jalopy. Both traveled across the road and up a steep bank where Old

John fell back onto the hood. It took a lot of cussing and tugging to get that mule off the hood and untangled from his collar and harness. However, we got that garden plowed I do recollect. Anytime Old John neared that rattletrap Ford he would perk up his ears and roll his eyes like Satchmo Armstrong and give a little snort.

When we were living in Michigan, we had running water and a toilet. It was a poop-paper-flush-and-run toilet. But here at the Harris place we had to go outside to poop, and we wiped with paper ripped from a catalog. This required some training from Mom, who taught us how to take it and crumble it up, just so, and wipe. On a visit one morning I saw some fresh-shelled corn cobs down in the hole and, for a minute or two, I analyzed the perfect use for them. I too kept a stash handy. At certain times they just worked better than the tool section of the catalog.

The summer of '48 just seemed to be one adventure after another. When we were not helping Mom with the garden work, we would be exploring our new territory. One day baby Lois climbed up an old apple tree, losing her grip and falling. Lois's foot got wedged into the fork of a limb, and we tried and tried to get her unstuck. Mom was holding her up when Frank finally had to get a saw and cut the tree limb, muttering about having a bunch of ignorant offspring.

A big adventure for our collective family was a trip over to Bedford to buy apples at a large orchard. We all piled into Frank's old flatbed truck with Mom in the middle with the gearshift between her legs, Grandma Elsie ridin' shotgun, and all the rest of us climbing in the back. It was every bit of forty miles over there, so it was a wonderful tour running east on U.S. 50 of Indiana.

Often we bought extra apples for other family members who placed an order when they didn't come along to buy their own. It was a cheerful time coming back with big red apples in full wooden baskets or crates, and kids spaced in all around them. Frank instructed us not to eat any, less we wanted a good switching, but when Grandma got one from the basket—well heck!—our trail could easily be picked up from the apple cores left behind. It wasn't long, though, that a full tummy and the whine of them bald "tars" put us to a nice sleep.

There were other times when we had a flatbed foray. Like when we all went to pick blackberries. We would toss galvanized washtubs, milk buckets, and every little gallon tin we could find into the truck. We would make holes in the two sides of the tin and tie a strand of bailing twine or, even better, a piece of bailing wire to make a pail. Some of the pails we had were little gallon lard buckets that were ideal for the job.

Usually, we didn't ask folks for permission to pick berries along fence rows, edges of woods, or hillside pastures. We were like a bunch of dang locust coming through the place. It was, however, rather rural and isolated where we did our picking, and even Frank had enough sense to keep us hidden in the bush.

On one of those blackberry expeditions I learned another rather important technique in country life. We were moving down a weeded dirt lane that had trees on one side, high bushes on the other, and a little brook of water running alongside of the road. The flatbed stopped in a shady part of the road—a good place for everyone to relieve themselves.

It was little Tom's desire to go take a poop. So, with my recently acquired bibs, passed down from Ed, Gayle, and who knows where he inherited them from, I sashayed out behind a bush. I unhooked both straps and threw back the bibs, squatted, and let it rip. I improvised with bush leaves to wipe and stood up hurriedly flipping the back of my bibs up over my shoulders.

I felt the warm, clumpy, wetness roll down my back and splattering at the same time on the back of my head and neck—what to do? I

Chapter 2 - Harris House

guess from the look on my face and the fresh fragrance of Tommy poop, the others quickly realize the issue at hand. For the moment everything seemed a little blurred, between all the laughter, cussing, and "puuweees" going on.

The only reason Frank didn't slap me on the back of my head was that he didn't want poop all over him too. Mom got me out of my bibs and walked me down to the brook, where she washed me down and washed out the bibs. Once we got home, Mom showed me how to loosen bib straps and roll 'em down. I never soiled my bibs again.

As summer came to an end, the air got more crisp and the grass was pretty much dead. We brought in the unhusked popcorn, peppers, onions, and 'taters from the garden, and hung 'em up for winter storage. Frank was called back to the mine and the coal pile was being stocked up. My Uncle Everett married Aggie Patterson. From my room I could look about three quarters of a mile north and see that big old brick building we knew as school. It was September, and I was a seasoned six-year-old headed for the first grade.

Cannelburg, according to one historian, "sprang into existence" during the late 1870s because of the Buckeye Cannel Coal Company. Cannel coal was considered premium in the state, and Buckeye Company employed many men, including most of the town citizens. In fact, Cannelburg took the name from the coal, just like Cannelton, Indiana, and Cannelton, West Virginia. Even today old structures still sit on the foundation of blocks of cannel coal. Walkways, and even cellars, were laid up with cannel coal, which was whitewashed to make it brighter. The Harris House rested on blocks of cannel coal as well.

In 1881-82 a pandemic of small pox left a great number dead. The epidemic ravished a large number of children and this set the school back in its development. But by 1914 a new consolidated high school building was erected with all the modern improvements and educational equipment of the time. This was more or less the way it stayed for the next thirty some odd years.

There had been additions made over time, and one of my favorites was the fire escape placed outside on the south side. The escape was a metal cylinder starting at the top side and slanting downward to the ground with an outward double swinging door at the top. Many a noon hour the teachers let us (the lower grades) climb the stairs and slide down the escape. Sometimes we boys would try to climb from the bottom up, but it was always an avalanche when someone in the lead would lose his footing and take us all back down to the bottom. Over and over this was played. When the girls went sliding down they bunched up their dresses and kept their knees together—just a little observation I made. This metal gut was as slick as ice from all the kids that slid down it over the years. When we had official fire drills, the lower classes walked out. We linked up with the classmate in front and the one behind, and then formed blocks at our designated areas outside. However, the upper-room classmates slid down the escape with the teachers being the last out.

Between the basketball court and the ball field there sat a merry-go-round, a rack of swings, and a teeter-totter. Girls mostly used the totter, as I recall. The merry-go-round could be a rough game at times. We boys would run, push it as fast as our little legs were able, and then hop on. Someone always got dragged along because he mistimed the jump-on. The ball courts and the ball field were usually occupied by the upper-class boys.

The two-story brick structure had its offices upstairs, along with the music room with a piano that could be rolled out. The sixth-, seventh-, and eighth-grade rooms were located at topside too. A large assembly room was upstairs. We gathered here for special events, like a ventriloquist show, or some other sort of intrigue touring the area schools. All of the floors were wooden tongue and groove, except the coal and janitorial rooms. A sawdust and fine oil mix was laid down by Mr. Lavely, the school custodian, who would sweep this concoction across the floor, in an effort to keep life in the wood and control dust. From years of use, the stairs were worn in the middle and dished out smoothly, leaving a sanded appearance in the wood, displaying its grain. Every classroom, as I can recall, had windows on one side, and under the windows all the radiator heaters were lined up. These were steam heated from the coal-fired boiler that the janitor fired up early every morning.

 Many a day wet brown jersey gloves were stretched out over the radiators, and the musty smell of them drying out was common, along with the very noticeable and pungent smell of barnyard manure from the Amish boys' shoes, pants, and shirts. Their morning chore clothes were also their school clothes, and often fresh manure polished their shoes.

 Every classroom had massive slate blackboards with a chalk-and-eraser railing parallel to the floor at the bottom. Walk through the open door and the teacher's desk was always up front and to the center, whereas both walls, one behind the teacher and the other opposite the window wall, held the blackboards. One of my jobs was to take the chalk erasers outside and slap the dust out of them on the concrete stairway entrance. I should have had compensation for chalk lung. The A-B-Cs were displayed above and along the top of the blackboard, along with student artwork depicting specific seasons or events. The back wall had coat hangers, and under them were bookshelves. In one corner a painting of George Washington in the clouds looked down on us in a very somber way, and in the other corner an American flag on a staff stood with forty-eight stars.

Every single morning the desks could be heard screeching on the floor when the whole class would stand for the pledge of allegiance. Our desks were wooden and had an open compartment where we kept our "learning things." The top of the desk had a round inkwell at the top left-hand corner.

Every kid within a mile of the school walked or sometimes caught a passing ride. I walked along with my brothers, Gayle and Ed. We had our lunch in brown paper bags, or wrapped in newspaper, which was usually a fried egg sandwich and, if we were really lucky, some leftover pie. (Anything that was left over at one of our meals was more than likely not edible.)

Nearly half of the distance to school was Four Points. It was where Fox Road from the south met Cannelburg Road from the north, and U.S.50 stretched east to west, with stop signs on the north and south roads. Located there was a gas station owned by F.X. Wilson and grocery store maintained by his sister, Cecilia Wilson. (To my ear and from my tongue it was always Silya Wilson.) Going north the store was to our left and the station was to the right. F.X. and Cecilia lived in separate houses uphill, to the west of the stores. In the grocery store, she had a glass cabinet that held different lunch meats, sliced ham, pickle loaf, baloney, and various cheeses. Mom would let us go to the store at noon, where Cecilia would make us a sandwich. We washed it down with a pop, while sitting outside on a big red wooden box watching traffic go by.

Cecilia would put all these lunches on a tab, noting them on a little yellow pad. We got a lot of condiments for home from the store, and Frank was given a running tab as would most of the community. It was blasphemous not to pay it up, or some of it, every month. Even if we were frugal, Frank always thought we consumed too much, and you just knew a lecture about was forthcoming when the monthly tally arrived.

Chapter 2 - Harris House

My first grade was a delightful one, and my teacher, Miss Kunkler, was as kind and nurturing a teacher as I ever had. First grade was probably my greatest academic success. We just copied letters and learned numbers. With numbers I had a sharp pencil, and didn't do too bad, at least I wasn't so intimidated by them. It was easy enough to copy an A, B, and C as well. In fact, as I progressed in school, my most honed talent was copying.

It was a little daunting when we had the same letters put together, like C-A-T. This may have been the early hint that something wasn't quite right. But heck, there were little Amish kids who barely spoke English. The only thing up to now that they spoke or had heard was Dutch. (As I recall, the Amish girls never talked out loud, they just bunched up and whispered to each other.) So, from my perspective, we were all equally ignorant.

Toward midterm, my first streak of vanity occurred. I was able to look into a mirror and see the development of a young Tommy. First thing I took note of (and anyone else who observed did too) was that I had something of buck teeth, with a gap big enough between the two front teeth to pull an ear of corn through with nothing on the other end but a clean cob. Old John the mule's grin was fuller than my own. This was to be my only physical blemish. As far as I was concerned, no one looked as debonair. Even so, a few of my sidekicks seemed to glance in my direction when singing along to a hit song that year: "All I Want for Christmas Is My Two Front Teeth."

Christmas was not always the most pleasant occurrence for my family. Aside from a few special memories for me, it usually meant Frank being drunk or hungover, a family squabble, or a tirade by Frank before the day of good tidings came to an end.

In later Christmases, we boys bought Frank a carton of Camel cigarettes, his choice right up to the end, and he bought us hunting permits and ammo.

If he gave you seven rounds, he expected no less than five rabbits. One day, Frank and Uncle Everett went rabbit hunting, and he came back with five rabbits and a box of shot gun rounds with only five out. "See here this is how it's done." Mom told us later that he went through a whole box and five.

My first year as a scholar was on the down side and the thaw was in the ground. At the Harris House we were moving the winter pile of barn manure and slinging it over the garden. There were other things being slung about in my head too. For in school classmates were turning their reader pages rather quickly. To be sure, I wasn't the only slow one; but too often, I thought, I was being corrected for my confusion, and my thinking process mired down on a single word.

Take a word out of the box and lay it on the table and it seemed understandable. Hearing Miss Kunkler say it, and others say it, I understood it. Take that same word and put it back in the box with all the others, well, geez, it took a whole different appearance. I'd chew on that for a while, skip it, and go on to the next word. It was like skipping a stone across water, I'd go to the next word that I did recognize, and then try to rationalize what everything meant in between. And so it went for the rest of the term. The whole time I kept a well-tuned ear to what was being said by the fast page turners; this enabled me to stay with "the story."

Well, that first year wasn't all so bad. I acquired sufficient enough smarts to be passed on to second grade, and I found that I rather enjoyed school.

Decoration Day 1949, a day set aside like no other during the year. The Harrawoods always honored Sgt. Paul Harrawood at his grave site.

Crippled and disfigured men attended grave yards everywhere with the American Legion, as did Veterans of Foreign Wars members, with "barrack caps" placed jauntily on their heads, Red Poppies in their lapels, and whiskey on their breath.

The names of the war dead were read out loud, and at every mention of a name there was a mom or a dad, a brother or a sister, a son or a daughter, or a wife who let escape, from deep inside of their soul, a sobbing moan of loss. The post chaplin would give a prayer, and a song, "Nearer to thee…," would trail off across the graves. The seven rifle-carrying Legionnaires would stand in rank, and once the command was barked, twenty-one rifle shot reports echoed across the landscape. Then the long sad notes of the bugler playing "Taps" began: dah dah daaah. DAH DAh Daaah … At the conclusion, salutes were made, handshakes given, hugs, and tears dried away. Young boys scrambled to search the cemetery lawn for the expended brass cartridges ejected from the rifles. Everyone would get in their automobiles; some would go home, and others would follow the Veteran's parade on to the next graveyard where a mom and a dad were waiting.

This day was the start of summer, and if you had a good ear, you could pick up the greatest spectacle in car racing, the Indianapolis 500, drifting out from the windows of folk's homes. For us it was also "tater planting time." (Well, according to Grandpa, it went: Plant 'em, Decoration Day, and dig 'em up Labor Day.) The popcorn, tomatoes, and peppers were planted in the ground, and the white blossom of the blackberries sprinkled across the country side. It excited any boy enough to get his cane pole out and do some fishing. Mom would cut up some pokeweed, throw in a little bacon, and make up some greens. In a big ol' cast iron skillet, mushrooms and bluegill fish would fry, and this was all curtained over by the earthy smell of sassafras tea brewing.

Not everything off Mom's cook stove was tasty. One day I ran into the house and on the cook stove was a big crock of mashed potatoes. I gripped the ladle beside it and helped myself by taking a big bite. Mom was out hanging clothes on the line when I came out and told her "the mash 'taters wasn't very tasty."

"Mash 'taters," mom said. "What mashed potatoes are you talking about?"

"The ones on the stove," I replied.

"That's not potatoes," mom said. "That's starch."

It wasn't too bad eating a big gulp of starch, except for the stiff neck it gave me.

As time went on, my summers were not much different than my first at the Harris House. The apple trips over to Bedford were as delightful as the first. Blackberry picking was okay, but eventually it started feeling more like a job, rather than an exciting time. However, there was a new twist in picking berries though, and that was when we started going to the "strip pits" to wash off and swim.

The pit was essentially a cellar cut made by a dragline. The overburden was slung over to one side, making the spoil piles (some called them coal banks). A bulldozer would make a graded lane leading down to the face of the coal seam. Here a steam shovel loaded it in trucks and hauled it out of the pit. (Steam shovels were falling to the past, as they were quickly being replaced by diesel-powered engines.) The pit continued until the seam played out or the mine property ended. Then, either the mine started over alongside of the old pit, spoiling into it, or left the empty pit and moved to a new lease. The rain and water runoff filled them up in no time, making a clear swimming hole, though often with a sulfurous taste and providing a slight burn to the eyes.

Chapter 2 - Harris House

It was a wonderful time at the pits. Because of their structure, there was a shallow end, where you could simply walk right into deeper water without any quick drop off. Or you could climb along the high wall and make a running jump into the water a few feet below. Swimming and bathing was a dual purpose trip to the pits. And the whole combined Harrawood family would, again, pile on to Frank's old flat bed, loaded with patched up inner tubes and bars of Ivory soap.

Women of the family would strip down to under clothes, reach in under their bras and wash up really good, then duck down under the water as many times as it took to feel clean. Ivory soap would float, so when a request came from someone, "throw me the soap," it could be tossed without fear of being lost. I can still see the bits and pieces of Ivory soap floating along the edge of the pits. The women might get out and towel dry themselves, and comb out their hair. Or they might sit on a rock and sun. Or they might just float out further in the deep water on the tubes. The men folk sometimes would see who could swim across under the water. Some of the older boys would leap from the high wall trying to jump through an inner tube, making sure that the valve stems face safely downward! The little fellers stayed where they could always touch the bottom with their little white dolphin-like butts rolling in the water. We all learned to swim in these pits, even if it was dog paddling. These were sacred swim holes, and they were jealously guarded even though we didn't own them (seldom were we prohibited from them). My family and all my boyhood friends enjoyed our strip pits for many years.

There are two incidents that quickly come to mind that happened at the strip pits. The new home that Uncle Everett built was just east of the old Harris House. He and Frank built a small milking barn with a hayloft and a corn crib on the side. Inside of the crib Everett had an old gas mask hanging on the wall. Relics from the war were found scattered around in out buildings almost everywhere. Many a time, I would ask Everett for that mask, with him always refusing. Eventually he surrendered and finally said, "Okay you can have the darn thing." Oh joy, I had conceived a great plan for that mask.

Uncle Everett was my hero. I was so fascinated that he had been a Navy frogman. Many a time, when the cornstalks in the fields towered above my head, I held my carved wooden knife in between my teeth and some sort of makeshift diving mask on my head pretending to be under the water. I fought Japs, Germans, and giant clams.

But now…oh boy, oh boy, I had a mask. I got some tape and taped up any possible place water might enter. Then I made an intake device from a garden hose. Now I needed the assistance of Jim and Ed. I divulged my plan and they both readily volunteered to assist me on my quest. I lifted about ten feet of garden hose and attached it to the mask. I made a dry run, placing the mask on, and had Jim and Ed blow into the mask. Eureka! I felt air rush in through the hose and into the mask. We headed for the strip pits. My brothers and I discussed all the possibilities, and if it did work, well, who would have the next turn. All of us were quick stepping to get to the water.

We made one more dry run and, other than my mask fogging up, it worked just "hunky dory." It was time to submerge. I gave thumbs up for my brothers, who were blowing in the hose. I waded out to where I could get down in enough water, but my buoyancy and the hose made it so I was more in a prone position. Going down to the bottom and pointing to shore, I submerged. In my head I heard the "dive, dive," horn you hear in all the war movies. I heard my breathing and then I was under. Boy howdy, I was under! I was under with no water seeping in and breathing fine, when suddenly I felt a warm liquid filling the mask, and a terrible stinging in my eyes. I came to the top ripping off the mask. Jim and Ed were peeing down the hose.

Another event occurred south of us where a local boy from Washington was swimming with others. He went under but never came up. When a police car traveling at high speeds passes through the country with a parade of cars following, including an ambulance, one does not wonder what is going on; one investigates and joins the parade. That's how we ended up at the strip pit. Uncle Everett was there along with Aunt Aggie. (And who didn't know that he was a frogman?) Everett made some quick shallow dives but without success. Someone produced an oxygen tank from the ambulance, and Everett put the mask up to his face. Aggie suggested he do otherwise. The old frogman slipped in under the water holding the tank in one hand and the mask tight to his nose and mouth. It wasn't that long at all before he popped out of the water coughing, hacking, and gasping; he nearly drowned. That was it for the attempt at a rescue. The pit was one of the deeper in the area, nearly sixty feet. The pit was dragged and the unfortunate boy was found sometime later.

The water table in our area was not a reliable source; good wells were a rarity. That's why most every home had a cistern. Cannelburg had a deep well and it was the community well. In dry periods water in cisterns and shallow wells went dry. On summer evenings locals showed up at the well. They would carry jugs, tall dairy milk cans, or any suitable container to haul water. Cars, pickups, and even the horse and buggy of the Amish gathered around the well. No one fussed about who was next in line, as everyone knew who or what containers were next. In earlier years, the Red Jacket pump was attached to a windmill and pumped into a tank. But now it had to be hand pumped directly into our containers. This was a time when we kids would romp around with each other. Even when we got our fill of water the kids and adults often stayed around and visited.

At home we would take a bath in tubs, especially during the dog days of summer. We were warned not to get in the pits or farm ponds because you might catch "polio." Still it was hard to keep us out of the water during hot summer days. Nonetheless, at bath times, there was an ascending order: first, baby Lois, then Jimmie, then me, then Ed, then Gayle, after whom the water was rationed out on the garden and new water poured in for Mom and Frank.

Going to the movies was a favorite entertainment of ours. Mom liked the movies as much as us boys, and we worked in unison to pick up enough cash to buy our way into the Ritz Theater at Loogootee. When I say picked up enough cash, I'm being literal. I would stand on the running board of Mom's old Model A and Ed would be on the other side (we were the pick-up men), while Mom would slowly drive down the roads searching the roadside for discarded pop bottles. At two cents a bottle on returns, five bottles each got you inside the theater. If we still didn't have enough, we would go down to Four Points, buy a pop (on credit, of course), and cash in on the bottles.

Then there were the free movies at Montgomery that we made a sure practice of attending each Thursday evening. This theater was not as fancy as the Ritz in Loogootee; movies were shown on the side of a big brick building. In preparation for the free show, we popped big bags of corn and filled jugs with ice tea or Kool-Aid. The bags of popped corn became saturated with the bacon grease that we popped it in, and by the time we got to the free movies the grease was oozing from the bag.

We loaded up in the old flatbed truck with Mom, who drove, Aunt Aggie, Uncle Everett's wife, and Aunt Laura Rose, who rode up front. (I want to take a moment here to say that Aunt Aggie was one of the sweetest ladies I have known. I loved and respected her dearly, and she was my mother's closest friend.) The movie was flashed up on the old Harris and Bell building, a five-story flour mill. Folks attending would spread blankets over the pavement or unfold wooden chairs, and kids gallivanted about the area. The movies were of the usual serial episodes. You know, the wagon with the good guys and pretty girl were chased by the bad guys and everyone goes over the cliff. Movie ends. Next time the good guys with the pretty girl, as it turns out, were saved because they were able to jump off just in time.

During intermission the reel would be changed and pop, candy, or various other refreshments could be had at Lum and Edwards's store, if you had the money.

Sometimes we were fortunate enough to go to the East 50 Drive-In. Its location was about half way between Montgomery and Washington. As usual, it was Mom who would take us. We all would sit down in front of the projector and concession building. Down in front of the great wood-framed screen was a park-like area. There we played on swings and slides. The biggest thrill was riding a miniature train whose rails were laid down in a circle and which traveled behind and under the great screen. This kept us occupied until it was dark enough for the cartoon to start. I recall the ghost-like flickering of the projected light over our heads and the night bugs that were attracted to the light.

Later, when I was older, the Russell boys and I would hitchhike to the drive-in. We came in from the surrounding corn field and sneaked in under the fence. When our luck failed to catch a ride back, we had a good ten miles to walk back home. It might be two o'clock in the morning getting back home, but no one really missed us anyway.

At sixteen I was able to drive myself to the drive-in with the money that I was making as a farm hand. The, "passion pit" presented some of the best times for us cornfield rebels. Always, if you didn't have a date, there was the thrill of the chase to find some girl to "make out with." Just as there were cars of boys, there were also cars of girls.

Alas! Summer again gave way to the shorter days, and before you could hear Frank say, "it was getting as cold as a banker's heart," the garden crops were in, canning jars filled, farmers were picking corn, and I was seven years old headed into second grade.

CHAPTER THREE

The Scholar

My brothers and I walked over to Cannelburg many times and watched the passenger trains go east and west on the B&O railroad. It was amazing to watch the postmaster hang a mail sack on a hook, waiting for a roaring train to come along. A railroad man inside the train would lean out with a long pole and snatch the bag. We played on top of the wooden box cars on the side rail switch, jumping from one to the other on down the line. We hugged tight when trains, rumbled by, rocking us and the empty cars. We were warned by Frank not to play on those boxcars; and besides, a hobo might get us. "Yeah, sure!" In fact, we were hoping that we would encounter a hobo. Playing here in town acquainted us with lots of the town boys and girls who became longtime friends. This is especially true with Gary Love whose life story I will touch on later.

There were always some new faces when we started back to school, but we recognized most everyone from town and a few from out our way giving us some reassurance. Nothing, otherwise, seemed unchanged to me. The classroom looked much like the first grade room. The teacher assigned us our desks in an alphabetical formation. Roll call sounded something like this: "Graber, Graber, Graber, and Harrawood."

We put our new school supplies in our desks. I loved the smell of the new writing tablets and especially liked the big picture of the Indian chief on the front. I fingered my big black writing pencil and the square chunk of rubber eraser. I knew that we were going to be serious scholars when Miss Hunter began with numbers on the blackboard. The first week it all went smoothly with Miss Hunter's writing on the blackboard. We would copy on our tablets. The assignment was to keep our writing in between the lines, and that wasn't always the easiest thing for me to do. During part of the day we would do numbers. Then we would do letters. Then we would put letters together and match them up with a picture in one of our readers and say the word that the letters made. Miss Hunter would hold up a picture and say, "Linda, what is this?"

And Linda would say, "A cow."

Then Miss Hunter would ask, "Linda, how do you spell cow?"

Linda would say, "C-O-W, cow."

Recess came and we started right where we ended last year with the merry-go-round. Before the merry-go-round made a full revolution I had already forgotten how to spell cow.

I was somewhat efficient with the pig, cow, dog, and cat thing; not so hard to match that up with a picture. This was going to be better than I imagined. As I loosely recalled, we already did this in first grade. However, we were moving through this exercise rather quickly. Teacher then threw a fast curveball at us. She started asking us to spell something without the pictures, and they were no longer the three-letter assortment. Words like tree, rain, snow, shoes, and so on started popping up. She kept talking about vowels and syllables. What the heck were those? That wasn't the half of it. Now we were not only spelling, but also writing what we were reading and being asked by teacher to read OUTLOUD! I didn't like where this was going one bit.

Lightning struck me twice in Miss Hunter's classroom one day. "Tommy," she asked in her sweet but authoritarian voice, "spell apple."

Where the hell did that come from? Sure, we were talking apples.

Chapter 3 - The Scholar

Like two apples from six apples would leave how many? But I sure as heck don't remember this being a required spelling word. Well, what the heck, I started, "Apple…uh…H—ooh—," there was a burst of giggles, "Uh—Hap-o-paw-al," I slowly stretched out the word, impressing my teacher no doubt. The giggles went to laughter, and so I gave a big toothy-gapped grin back, and lo! There was even more laughter.

"Okay, Tommy, you may sit down. Linda, spell apple."

"A-P-P-L-E, apple." She rattled it off like a clatter bone in a goose's ass. (A phrase Frank often would resort to when describing the character of someone besting him in an argument.) Well, I was getting around to spelling it but the teacher just cut me short. It was time for recess anyway.

Back from recess, we were asked to get out our readers. The shuffling and thumping of kids taking their books out of their desks quieted down. Teacher took her pointer in one hand and her reader in another hand and pointing to a classmate asked them to read. One of my buddies might stumble on a word or one of those "sillyaboles," and every one would giggle, (even me), but he'd never stumble on that word again.

Now, me, I would try to disappear, never daring to make eye contact with the teacher. "Tommy?" she inquired. What Tommy, I thought, there ain't no Tommy here. Second lightning strike!

"Tommy, please continue to read." Read? I didn't even know what page we were on. I was too intent on listening to the story, and there was no way I was able to follow someone reading. Do something quick Thomas Earl, I thought to myself. I shoved my book off the desk, making it look like an accident, of course. There were a bunch of giggles and I grinned big, which brought more giggles. "I, uh, lost the page we were on Mrs. Hunter," I replied in the most regretful tone.

"Page six, Tommy, we're on page six." No way out—think, think.

"Page one," I turn to the next page… real slow… "Page two," I did a quick look around the classroom and flashed my grin, which resulted in a burst of laughter. "Page three," I continue on.

Teacher, a bit exasperated, said "Okay, Tommy you may sit. Linda, will you continue to read please." Saved again by the smart clatter bone.

I was absolutely struck with fear to demonstrate my reading ability. Because, even alone with no one around, I tried to interpret those silly looking things called words. I just looked for something that I recognized that clued me in on what the story might be. No matter how hard I tried I simply could not bust out of this word prison.

Back then, education in Indiana was in a transitional phase. There were still a few single-room schools scattered about but, for the most, the desks in these one-roomers remained vacant. A battle between the state legislatures, professional teachers' organizations, and centers of higher learning had long fought the township trustee, who for years controlled the education of each township. Trustees set the wages and hired the teachers, who most likely went no further than the eighth grade themselves. They decided what texts were to be used and even decided the curriculum to be taught. Trustees often looked out more for themselves than their schools, but as politicians they reflected the likes of the township folks.

What the township people wanted was low taxes, no intrusion from the outside, and essential home rule. What educators wanted was a professional tenured teacher under a hierarchical system. Moreover, they wanted these township schools shut down and a countywide system put in place. Basically, they sought a consolidation of schools guided by a single controlling interest. They got some of that but not all of it. Through legislatures and voter pressure from the 1920s to the 1950s, something of a compromise was made. Bus routes were created, the state increased the moneys for rural schools, and education was now provided by certified state teachers.

Chapter 3 - The Scholar

Schools in towns like Cannelburg were updated to meet testing requirements and, overall, a more equitable standard between these rural schools and the larger city schools. The one thing, however, that didn't change was the mistrust of state control, higher taxation, and the resolute pride in community schools and basketball teams. And, no matter how much increased pressure there was from Indianapolis for consolidation of schools, it was not going to be "our school" that would lose out.

That's why the Cannelburg "Mud Daubers," the Epsom "Salts," the Odon "Bulldogs," the Plainville "Midgets," the Montgomery "Vikings," the Elnora "Owls", the Glendale "Bears", the Burn City "Bees," the Scotland "Scotties," the Alfordsville "Yellow Jackets," and the Washington "Hatchets," to name a few, were not about to fold their flags.

Cannelburg School was not bending from the winds of new teaching theories either. There were no considerations for anything like a special class for slow learners—nothing of the sort. If a student didn't get it the first time, they were left behind, and if after the second time they were still marginal, well, just pass them on. Soon enough they'll turn 16. There were a few students who were left behind more than once in separate grades. I had a friend who joked that by the time he graduated from high school he was able to drop by a tavern for a beer on his way to class.

Now, a learning disability like mine was being examined by the philosophizers and big universities elsewhere, to be sure, but here in little old Cannelburg and Miss Hunter's classroom, dyslexia might as well have been a new found distant planet. Here at the Cannelburg school the three R's—Reading, Riting, and Rithmetic—taught to the tune of a hickory stick established the education theory.

It became a long blur my second year. Linda was reading faster than I could think. I was pulling off antics that gained the attention and laughter from my fellow classmates when called on by Miss Hunter to read, spell, or solve math; I didn't realize the importance of test scores at this point. After all, I was, in all sincerity, trying to do my best and according to Tom's little brain that was good enough.

That year, Thanksgiving was celebrated at my grandparent's farm. Then Christmas came and left, leaving everyone singing about Rudolph the Red-Nosed Reindeer. And I was on the other side of being a second grader. Preoccupied by the warm spring sunshine and robins dancing on the outside window ledge of the classroom, it came as no shock to me that I was failing. Quite simply, neither it nor the meaning of "not promoted" meant anything to me.

Second grade second time

I didn't feel much remorse about not being promoted to the third grade. School was out, summer was in, and I celebrated my eighth birthday. Summer more or less became a routine: playing on the box cars in Cannelburg with my buddies; picking up soda bottles; going to the free movies; and doing the home chores.

Frank hauled all the kids down to Great Uncle Chet's farm. Chet and Alice Gregory had as many girls as we boys, so we had plenty of the kid camaraderie that you can have when visiting. We were led on expeditions around the farm by our second cousins. We scaled the hayloft ladder and tossed and tumbled in the soft hay. We also skipped stones across the farm ponds; fed the newborn colts; and picked and ate ripe, tart gooseberries while being serenaded by a cacophony of guinea hens.

Once when an old buggy caught our attention, it became apparent that the Gregory girls had a game in mind. The buggy was pulled to a sloping pathway. Gayle, Ed, and all but one of the girls got into the buggy. I wanted to be a passenger, but they claimed that it would be overloaded.

Chapter 3 - The Scholar

The buggy was given a little shove by one of the girls who then jumped on. The buggy first moved at a snail's pace, then picked up speed, and eventually coasted to a stop, and the riders would pull the buggy back up to the top and do it again. Still they refused to let me ride. So, with my strategic mind, I positioned myself down trail at the point where the buggy would be at its full speed. I picked a great ambush site. When I heard laughter and saw the zooming buggy pop over the rise, that's when, with strength emboldened by shear cunningness, I picked up a log and tossed it in the pathway. The buggy flipped up and over, spilling its passengers out over the pathway like a bunch of bumble bees tumbling out of a nest. When they regained their senses, I was chased by the vigilantes for the rest of the day. When they finally captured me, they were all too exhausted to commence the execution.

  The impact of summer's end soon came to me. I was walking toward the school. Clasped in one hand was the handle of my new Roy Rogers lunch bucket with a thermos filled with milk, swinging to my rendition of "R-A-G-G…M-O-P-P… Rag Mopp," a well-liked tune at the time and perhaps the only word I was certain of its spelling. I don't remember having apprehensions of what I was jauntily heading toward. I started a review of last year in my head. No intimidation of having a new teacher; Miss Hunter would still be there. I was already familiar with the reader I would be using; it was right where I left it when school let out. My color crayons were mostly intact and I had a new arsenal of pencils. I even had a few new clothes to wear.

  As I approached the school house I started recognizing my old friends out on the playground. I cut through the basketball court and fell in with them. We reexamined our exploits during the summer and shared any gossip a third grader would have to divulge. That's when the school bell rang and I followed my school gang into the building. I walked into the class room with my buddies, but an outstretched arm caught me. It was the third grade teacher, Miss Donahue. "Tommy," she said in a civil tone. "You belong over there in that room." She turned me and gave me a gentle directional shove.

I couldn't have been smacked up the side of the head any harder. I had just learned the meaning of "left behind." A hail storm of emotions rained down on me as I walked into Miss Hunter's classroom. Like an automaton I headed right to my desk. Miss Hunter didn't bother to reassign me. I was back in the old saddle again. I knew it was mine for certain. My initials were carved in it from last year when Linda the clatter bone was reading.

I was a statistic for 1950. The illiteracy rate was 3.2 per cent. I must say, as I sat there looking around at the new faces, I had an urge to run for it. I felt the humiliation, the utter fear of having to interpret the words, the anguish at trying to write down words in a spelling test even as the next one was being given. I looked around for some familiar faces and I saw no other veterans. I was it. The rest of the day we organized ourselves through the instructions of Miss Hunter.

The first couple of weeks we reviewed the last part of the first grade and I did have a bit of shine here. I kept turning ahead in the speller and the reader book looking for things that I was familiar with. After all, this was plowed ground for me and I knew where the wet spots were. The time arrived when my tribulation would begin and that is, as I well understood, when second grade reading and spelling really started.

It was a Monday. We were about to begin the reading session. A commotion by some kid was creating quite a ruckus. Echoes of tortuous sounds came down the hallway from the fourth grade room. We detected the voices of two male adults and the panther-like screams of the kid. The voice of one adult and the panther kid had a familiar ring. The hallway storm was coming right to the second grade classroom.

Chapter 3 - The Scholar

Miss Hunter seemed not to be too alarmed with this turbulence, as if she expected it. The classroom door was already open. The anticipation of what was about to spring on these second graders had them shuffling about in their desk, but I was seasoned to this sort of thing. It happened at least once a week at home with Frank and us kids … FRANK!

Frank came through the door dragging Gayle, and on the other side of Gayle was the principal. Gayle may as well have been going to the electric chair, or at least that's what it seemed like. He was fighting as if it was his last day on earth—swinging his arms loose from the clutches of his antagonist; grabbing at the door jams; bracing against the door jamb; kicking, scooting, screaming, spitting, biting… (Did my brother have hydrophobia, I wondered.) But, of course, the second graders were wide-eyed with jaws dropped. Some even scrammed toward the back. Frank and the principal actually carried Gayle to a desk. Books were being scraped off desktops as this melee move on. Finally, Gayle was fastened down in his desk by the principal. Frank gave a big exhale and told Gayle to "sit there and learn." The principal stayed in the room standing next to Gayle during the reading period. Who said Frank never participated in his boys' education?

And that was that. Gayle had been shanghaied back here from the fourth grade to reinforce his ability to read. Only during reading session would he be in the second grade. The next few days Gayle sat there like a Buddha. Good gosh, I thought to myself. What in the heck waits for Tom? I can't say I remember Gayle and I ever discussing the merits of fine literature together during this time, but before mid-term, Gayle no longer attended second grade reading class.

I don't know if Miss Hunter held any aspirations for us. I am certain she thought she would never have two of these in her classroom at the same time. She had just sent Gayle on and then Ed. What she must have thought when she looked down the hall knowing that in the first grade another one, Jimmie, had been planted.

The school year chugged on like that little train—"I think I can, I think I can," and I was the caboose. Let me reiterate how sickening to the psyche it is when you are asked to read and your heart and soul is poured into the effort. Regardless of the teacher admonishing those students who laughed at my attempt, there were always the giggles when I got shipwrecked on a word. This dropped over me like a wet blanket of embarrassment. The old "drop the book" routine was past its sell-by date, and the silly antics displayed while standing in front of the class was good for a laugh, but never covered my inadequate abilities. A great sense of relief prevailed when I noticed that my teacher wasn't calling on me any more to read. It was even a greater relief when something of a revelation came about that not only the teacher but also the students realized that I had some sort of disability. After all, handsome Tom showed too much wit and tenacity in trying to accomplish the task. That reading dog just wouldn't hunt for me.

Being left behind and Gayle's ordeal haunted me to the point that I resorted to being as resolute to the cause as I could. The cause: I must do it my way; the school way is not getting it done. I started copying in every way my deviously inspired brain would let me. There's a big world out there waiting for me and I was not going to spend the rest of my life in this classroom.

I created a plan of action. A few examples: I would set my spelling book (folded in a position that I could readily shift it) inside the desk where I could glance down through the ink well during a test. I would break the lead of my pencil and go to the pencil sharpener. On the way up and on the way back a quick fly over and I could gain enough intelligence to make the necessary corrections when I got back to my desk. On differ-

Chapter 3 - The Scholar

ent occasions I had accomplices who slid their paper in such a way for me to make a mental swipe.

I was polite and asked in the most, "old buddy, buddy" way if I could lift some answers…and panicked when someone covered up their paper. The thought of intimidation never occurred to me, but it apparently did to others. Charlie, who sat next to me in class, usually let me steal his answers. Years later I had a chance to ask Dr. Charlie why he let me copy. "Because I was afraid you'd beat me up" was his reply. There was no humor in his voice.

There was one time when I remarkably passed a spelling test. Teacher graded our papers and handed them back the next day. I took a double take, "sawdust in my lunch pail," as I'd heard Uncle Everett say; I had a big red C+ on it. The teacher pulled the rug right out from under me though when she elaborated on how well we all had done and that we may keep our papers as this wasn't counting toward our overall grade. But Frank and Mom never knew that…even a blind hog gets an acorn every so often.

Good times at recess generally shook the drudgery off. I would meet up with my buddies who had gone on to third grade; no amount of pride or shame scuffed our friendship. We carried on with our recess frolics. The days were warm and the balls and bats coming out of the locker indicated an approaching end of school.

The spring peepers in the little pond between Four Points and home seemed to be singing out the announcement: "Tommy passed, Tommy passed." I was headed to the third grade.

That year, my family participated in the annual Decoration Day ceremonies and a VFW picnic. The family had great concern for Uncle Everett. He was reactivated into the Navy and was to report to Great Lakes on May 16. Since that day he had been doing every possible thing to secure a deferment. We were all holding our breath and waiting. It certainly seemed to us that Everett and the Harrawood men had gone above and beyond the call of duty for their country. This was all discussed while studying an atlas somebody produced to see just where this place called Korea was located.

Grandma Elsie harbored bitterness toward those men who finagled their way out of the war that ended five years ago. In her front window she still displayed three silver stars and one gold one. Especially brewing in the community was the rub that the Amish were hiding behind the skirts of religion, claiming exemption because they were conscientious objectors to war. This Korean War was not exactly what V-E and V-J days promised for the future. As a nine-year-old boy I clearly sensed the animosity brewing in the community. The war scares for our family abated when Uncle Everett received his Naval Speed Letter that 'deferred indefinitely [Everett]…from active military service', late in April. War and "commies in the government" conversations from within the family kept my ears perked throughout the summer.

"The caissons go rolling along…"

A most fascinating event happened early that summer. For three days a U.S. Army convoy moved west on U.S. 50. Trucks full of men in their olive drab uniforms drove by—trucks with taut tarpaulins over their beds—leaving my imagination to run wild. I saw trucks pulling artillery and lots of jeeps, some with long whipping antennas tied over the front with mounted machine guns. Others were pulling trailers and water tanks. Enclosed trucks with big red crosses on the side and over the tops of the cabs passed by. There were trucks with big guns mounted on them, big army green semi-trailers hauling green bulldozers and road graders, and still they kept coming. I sat on Cecilia's big red wooden box nursing soda pops and wondering for three days what communist invasion must be coming our way. I gave a big toothy grin and saluted often to the army guys as they rolled on.

I mentioned earlier that my only physical blemish was my front teeth. My Aunt Lois in Michigan volunteered to have them fixed. So Mom and I headed up to Aunt Lois's house, and she set up an appointment. After the dentist finished prying around inside my mouth, his appraisal suggested a cost of twelve hundred dollars! I didn't go home empty handed though—Aunt Lois bought me a used bicycle instead.

Frank and Uncle Everett were working a lot of overtime, in fact it just seemed to me that everyone was coming and going to work that summer. I rode my new used bike to work, too. Farmers needed a kid to steer tractors in between the rows of square hay bales as the bigger guys pitched 60 to 80-pound bales up on the wagons. When one wagon was stacked, I would get on another tractor and start all over. When both wagons were stacked, I climbed to the top of the stacked bales on the wagon and rode. The farmer or an older boy drove into the barnyard where the wagons pulled in under the big top door that had been let down. There may have been a tractor already on the other side of the barn or one of the field tractors was unhitched and used. (Sometimes a team of horses was used.) The tractor hitched to a rope backed up, easing the forks down from the loft. Men then hooked hay tongs into the square bales. Once the signal was given the tractor moved forward, slowly lifting a half dozen or more bales up to the door that led into the hayloft onto a horizontal track the full-length of the barn. Another signal was given and someone who held the trip line would pull hard and the hay would be released. The boys that stacked the wagons were the same that stacked in the loft. The tractor would be backed up and the forks dropped back on the wagon, as many times as it took to unload it. Then, with the empty wagons, we headed back out to the field. Sometimes we double-hitched wagons, and sometimes we passed a crew that was coming in as we were going out. It really depended on the farmer and how deep his pockets were. It was in these hay lofts and out there on those stacked wagons that I began learning from the more experienced guys about how to…well, things about the birds and bees that I always suspected, but wasn't totally sure about.

I worked at hay-making for years and in the beginning made three dollars a day. I evolved from the driver to the stacker to the tripper. At times I mowed, raked, and even made the bales. I realized farmers came to trust me, to a certain point anyway, and that boosted my self-esteem.

Esteem aside, the best thing about hay-making was the feast the farmer's wife (and, we always hoped, farmer's daughters) put on the table at noon hour. Absolutely the finest meals I ever ate, and it was washed down with the sweetest iced tea imaginable.

Summer was over for us school kids even though we tried to put it out of our minds. Those yellow buses going in for their inspections constantly reminded us that it was inevitable. And before you could say "Heartbreak Ridge," I was sitting at my third grade desk.

In the four years of school, I wised up to the review that would come in the new school year. However, I pondered briefly that there was no review for me this year. I acquired some extra books though. Arithmetic! At first I was familiar with numbers lined up in horizontal or vertical lines, and I understood the plus and minus signs. I did still have all ten fingers so I could do a little "add'n and subtract'n"; but way too soon the numbers came in short story form. "If Johnny gave three of his friends two pieces of candy, and Johnny still had two pieces left, how many pieces of candy did Johnny have to begin with? Right then and there I pretty much came to understand that I was dead in the water. How the heck can you solve a problem if you can't read it?

I had one option—cheat at every opportunity. And that's what I did. The teacher knew, and the classmates also knew it. To the right sat a smarter guy, a good buddy. In front sat a smart girl, and behind me another buddy a whole lot more skilled than me. And, miracle of all miracles, to the left of me was Dr. Charlie. Okay, the perimeter looked good, and the pencil sharpener was located in a good position. And that's how I got through the third grade.

A new learning adventure in the third grade was music class. We were trying to be taught a "do-re-mi" sort of thing, or "Every-good-boy-does-fine" sort of thing. And over and over we sang, "Jimmy crack corn and I don't care. Jimmy cracked corn and I don't care." I couldn't keep my pie hole shut. I asked teacher, "If Jimmy cracks his corn and we don't care, then why the heck are we singing about it." I dodged the flying eraser.

It was the first report card period, and my card showed negative results across the board. Frank decided it was time to teach me to read and, of course, he was well versed in the modern approach to teaching. After supper and the clearing of the dinner table, he took my reader and sat it down in front of me. He was generous enough to start at the first page.
He patiently asked me to begin reading. I started off then immediately got snagged on a word. Trying to muddle through that, Frank would slowly and very deliberately, in some phonetically abstract way, squeeze out the word. I took the cue and followed it. "Now, start at the beginning," he requested. From the beginning I recited and, approaching the word that we just stretched apart, I snagged on it again. "Dang it," Frank growled, and then would bellow out the snagged word. I would repeat and continue on reading. I'd read on into another hitch, and from Frank would come

another clear pronunciation. "Okay, start from the beginning," my stern taskmaster again requested. I read until I stumbled again, but now there was no clear articulation from him; it was a hard thump up against the head.

Ah, there it was! Now I was sure I would have a very delightful learning experience for the rest of the evening. Thump ... word ... thump ... word. At about ten that night Frank told me to go to bed as he was going over to his whiskey stash. To this day, I cringe when I try to make out a word. For the rest of my school days I never carried a book home. Far as that goes I never read a book either. Thus, my formal education, if you will, ended at the third grade.

There can only be one reason I was passed on: the school wanted to move me on as quickly as possible. The spring of 1952 introduced the first big wave of the baby boomers. There was no time to fuss with a marginal imbecile.

Wooden leg Willie

We had a genuine two-basket hoop on our court outside of Cannelburg School. The court was, indeed, regulation, running east to west, and we actually competed against rival schools. It did not have regulation markings, as it was understood, and everyone acknowledged the grass edge of the cinder covered court was out of bounds. Regulation games had referees, one from each school. We were unofficially known as the "Cannelburg Mud Daubers."

Basketball, being the state pastime as it was, was just a little too fast for Wooden Leg Willie to stay with the game. Willie didn't play basketball. He played softball.

Willie was of regular height to the rest of us boys. His face was splattered with freckles, and those freckles done a right good job of complementing his cayenne-pepper-colored, bowl-cut hair. Willie was an Amish boy, and we were good buddies in those days. Most Amish boys had a milk crock placed over the top of their head as a pattern for their haircut. The only thing that made Willie different from other Amish boys was Willie had a wooden leg.

It's not so unusual for people being hurt from horse-pulled implements, and the Amish used nothing but draft animals. It was hay mowing time, and the iron-seated mowing machine was being powered by a team of Belgians. The mowing machine was a steel-cleated, wheeled machine with a long tongue extending out for the harness hook up. As the team pulled the mower, a mesh of gears turned the five-foot sickle bar. The operator sat on an iron seat, controlling the levers to lock or raise the bar. This mechanism worked similar to a treadle-wheel sewing machine, only instead of vertically its action works flat. The sickles are literally razor sharp, and a well-maintained machine, swishing and making a methodic rhythm as it is being pulled through the hay field, can be a hypnotizing experience.

It would be anything but a pleasurable occurrence for young Willie. The team was halted, and for some reason the lock lever was not pulled back. Willie innocently stepped out in front of the mowing bar, and that's when the Belgians bolted, catching little Willie at the knee, zigzagging through his leg. Amish craftsmen devised a strapped wooden leg, which was shaped and modified often for Willie as he traveled through his boyhood.

Playing softball was a big thing for us boys, and our ball field was to the extreme west of our school. Nary a recess was absent of hitting flies, "Boston grounders," or just a game of throw and catch. The noon recess was when we had the big game, and Willie's leg never held us back from having him on our team. Willie was given a pass though. If he connected a reasonable enough base hit we gave him first, maybe even second. Sometimes he did make a homerun, and, as the stiff-legged Willie scurried around the bases, everyone would encourage him.

After the team at bat struck out three times and took the field, the other players coming in passed over their softball mitts. Willie, as an outfielder while waiting for a hit to come his way, would spin his straps and leg so that he could sit on his wooden leg like a milking stool. It was such fluid motion that it was like fine art to watch him bring that poplar made peg around when a ball came spinning his way. He always made the catch, and both sides would cheer for him. And so the game continued with the jeers, cat calls, and sometimes a heated provocation that led to a brawl.

Our schoolboys consisted of a lot of mixed tribes to a degree that it just couldn't be helped that disagreements turned into rubs, and, in many occasions, a fight. The town boys were mostly Irish and Catholic. A moniker given to them from the Amish and some Protestants was "cat lickers." Then there were the rural boys, some of them being Irish and Catholic themselves and, well, let's just say, a little meaner than their town cousins. The "fight'n style" varied as different as the boys there. The townies favored knuckled fist, but more of a slap than a punch, whereas the country boys fought like they were playing football, plunging right into the opponent (or opponents) and usually ending in something like a tussled match on the ground.

Amish had their style, too. Amish bishops in this particular settlement forbid the mule… just couldn't find that in the Bible…so I don't know how it was that they learned to kick like a mule and sashay around like dancing chickens, even their heads with their crock cuts bobbed like corks in a pond full of bluegill. Country boys, wise and fast to a good opportunity, quickly learned to catch a "kick'n bushhog" by his suspenders and send him a whirling out to the pitcher's mound.

Mr. Lavely, the school janitor, would pull his Bull's Eye pocket watch out from his bib pocket and check the time. Standing at the back entrance by the janitorial room, he would clasp the rope and tug at the recess bell to end the noon recess.

Back Words

and send him a whirling out to the pitcher's mound.

Mr. Lavely, the school janitor, would pull his Bull's Eye pocket watch out from his bib pocket and check the time. Standing at the back entrance by the janitorial room, he would clasp the rope and tug at the recess bell to end the noon recess.

Back Words

CHAPTER FOUR

The Smith House

Shortly after I muddled my way through the third grade, Frank found another fine home for us to live in, about twice the distance to school, south of the Harris House. This one went down in family history as the Smith House. It actually had a Smith living in it. I don't know why we left the Harris House or the arrangements Frank made with the frail old Mr. Smith. Maybe he convinced him that we would make home improvements or that we would take care of him. Whatever the case may have been, Mr. Smith had a room upstairs to himself, and we boys had the rest. After the first few months with all of us living there together, Mr. Smith packed up and high-tailed it out of there. We never saw him again.

By no means had we thought of ourselves as being poor. We understood what was poor. That distinction belonged to the family that moved in wherever we moved out. "The home is as sweet as a family makes it," or something like that, I've heard said. However, there was nothing sweet about us or the house we were moving out of, and it was not at all as charming a place as we were moving into. The obligatory can lids over mouse holes were present, and more would be tacked over. The ersatz wallpaper was there, as well as the ragged, sinking floor; the patched up roof; and outside, the rotten faded white-sided shingles, which were sagging. Shingles that were absent looked like missing teeth. Outside there was an outhouse. It, too, was sinking into a hole, but the hole was fairly deep, so that was a plus (in spite of the wasp nests). There was a barn and some sheds that seemed semi-functional. The chimney on the house roof looked floppy, but we never did check it thoroughly. The kitchen was a small closed in lean-to. We had to make shelves from concrete blocks to store canned goods. Groundhogs lived underneath it. Frank had really outdone himself this time.

You could strike a kitchen match and it would be blown out from the draft moving through the house. The electrification was even more basic than at the Harris place. The coal oil lamps were still a functional source of lighting for us. There was a cistern used for cooking and drinking water, and there was a well about a hundred yards from the house. It was sulfurous, stinking water that we used for baths only. We boys carried enough water to fill two tubs. We would take our baths, but instead of ascending order, the last one to take a bath now would be the first one next week.

All of us a little older and wiser, in makeshift homesteading, set to work. We made the chicken house secure enough to keep predators out, had a sow and her litter in a pen, and moved in a milk cow and her calf. Frank got this dehorned milk cow from hell, Old Betsy. She was the meanest cow any of us ever had to milk.

She functioned as our lawn mower, too, if you could call the perimeter of the house a lawn. The fencing was nearly gone, so we kept Betsy staked—and when I say staked, I should actually say anchored. She was tied to an old truck axle, and whenever anyone tried to get her she would buck and charge. One day Betsy caught Mom with her horn stubs in such a way as to give her a good tossing. Frank grabbed Betsy by the neck and was determine to break it. He twisted her until she flopped onto the ground with Frank underneath. Her legs pointed in one direction and her head in another, and Frank in a rage screamed "get off me."

When I'd get her by the lead she would drag me through hell and high water. Somehow, through a combined effort, she always got milked twice a day. We had her for about five years, but I was glad to see her made into hamburger.

A garden existed just south of the house, and it didn't take much to bring it back around. A deep creek meandered a bit to the north of the house, cutting back and heading west, then crossing under a bridge on Fox Road. By the bridge an old mine shaft and its shaken topside works, the tipple, sat on the same side of the road as the house. We were warned to stay away from this area, but at our first chance we made a bee line right to it.

One day we were tunneling into the slag pile by the shaft. I went down in the tunnel, and Jim and Ed jumped on top, collapsing it around me. Jim and Ed were trying to dig me out while smacking me in the head with the shovel. They both wrapped their arms around my head and shoulders, and began to tug. I could hear cracking sounds in my neck. When Frank was spotted coming toward us through the field, Jim and Ed who were covered in slag dust tossed me into the creek, clothes and all, to clean me up. Frank gave me some grief for being in the creek.

The whole place around there was wooly and grown over. There was a pond with one end being used as a trash dump and the opposite end overgrown with cattails. We would fight through this jungle just to get a swim even though it wasn't much deeper than three feet with heavy mud on the bottom.

We set box traps out to catch rabbits. Box traps were made just big enough for a rabbit to get into and closed on the other end. A hole on top and a shaft running down into the box held the bait. When the rabbit went inside, it tripped the rod leading back to the entrance and a sliding door would fall down trapping the cottontail. The rabbits were a mainstay for us. It was here at the Smith House that Grandpa gave me my first gun, which was a single shot, break over, 16-gauge shotgun.

Mom did her best to see that we enjoyed things of higher culture—things like taking us to the zoo in Evansville. This wasn't just a sudden decision; a trip like that had to be planned, and we knew when it was coming. Once, a day or so before going, Ed was standing on the top of a stepladder, and Jim and I pushed him over. Ed fell and smacked his head hard on the root of a maple tree. It coldcocked him good. He was blabbering senselessly and walking bizarrely. We were afraid that the excursion to the zoo wouldn't go as planned, so we put Ed in a tub and poured cold water over him to bring him back around. No one seemed to notice any difference in Ed, and we got to go to the zoo.

For years after we left the Smith House, you could observe an amber stain down the side of the outside wall. Its origin was from our upstairs window. At night when nature called, we would just pee through the screen. It was just too much trouble to go all the way downstairs and outside. I was still assigned the task of emptying the chamber pots, but this was a cold weather task. Even so, with a little body discipline, you could visit the outhouse early before bed and not have the "stinker muscles" move during the night so there was nothing to empty in the morning. A pee at night, however, just meant a quick trip over to the window.

When it came to peeing during the night, Jim didn't bother to go out or even go to the window. Jim peed in his bed. I guess it was unintentional. He was a bedwetter, so it was explained. But I was the one who shared the mattress with Jimmie, so I developed sleeping positions to avoid the leaching wetness.

There were days that it was absolutely necessary to haul that mattress down the stairs and outside to let it air out. The urine stains overlapping each other were reminiscent of a kaleidoscope pattern. If you drove by the house and glanced over at the mattress laying as it did, it looked like a bleached out decaying animal of some sort.

It wasn't easy to avoid noticing that Jimmie was overweight. Well, heck, he was just fat and that's all there was to it. Frank's favorite song that he sang to Jimmie was "Roly Poly, Daddy's Little Fatty." The rest of us boys called him "Girdle Stretcher." He often heard a little ode from us: "…fatty…fatty …two by four… so big you couldn't get through the bathroom door. So you did it on the floor." Jimmie had a speech impediment and it sounded sort of like this in his reply. "Do betta naugh tall may dat anye moor." It was during one of these mattress-airing-out days that the Russell boys visited and—boys being boys—we got into wrestling with each other.

The scuffle worked its way over toward the mattress when, in the heat of battle, Ed and I tossed Jack on the mattress without second guessing and then shoved Jim on top. Jack's arms and legs were now reaching for life from underneath Jim. Laying face up when Jimmie came crashing down on top, Jack's head was now under Jimmie. The mattress became something like a hotdog bun so that Jimmie couldn't get himself up. From my perspective, with Jimmie's chubby behind, and plump swells oozing out over Jack somewhere beneath it all, and with four arms and legs swinging wildly, Jack looked like a huge sand crab. That's when the flaying arms and legs of Jack begin to slow down and finally go limp. Working together, the Harrawood and Russell gang could barely get Jim off of Jack. We uncovered Jack, who had turned blue, gulping for air. In later years when we thought a rival fight might be coming our way, we always made sure Jim was standing between Ed and me.

It was at the Smith House that I really did have a chance to be a salvage diver. Not as heroic an adventure as Uncle Everett may have had, but it was just the same a thrilling deep dive recovery. It was one of those nights Frank worked late at the mine, but instead of coming home he headed to a bar. It was late and everyone was in bed. We all slept lightly when Frank was overdue coming home for we knew that it meant he would be returning home from drinking, and who the heck knew what disposition he'd be carrying.

It was late when we heard the truck come pulling in. The truck door opened…a short pause…truck door closed. Some shuffling on the gravel, Okay he's on the way to the outhouse. Then footsteps were on the porch…door opened. It wasn't that we didn't expect something to happen, anything could. But there was a period that gave us a little leeway and that was the step count from the door to his bedroom. If the count ended at his bedroom, then we could rest easy. But this night, the count passed his bedroom door and went right up the stairs.

Clump, clump, clump … those damn old number ten and a half Sears and Roebuck boots were mounting the stairway. Just from the tension bouncing off the walls, I knew I wasn't the only one wide awake. Don't move! It will give away your position.

One last chance. To the left Ed and Gayle's room and to the right Jim and…ah heck!

The blankets lifted off like a tornado had just passed over the bed. I was yanked out and thrown to the floor, landing on my behind. Before I could react to that, his iron-grip hand lifted me up from the floor. "What's the matter Dad?" and "What did I do?"

The aroma of whiskey and barroom smoke clung to his clothes, emitting a tinge of diesel fuel and a hint of shale dust. This, along with the copper taste of my own adrenaline, overwhelmed my senses for a slight moment.

"It's not what you did knot-head, it's what you're going to do," Frank replied, as I was bouncing down the stairs. The mystery deepened and the fear subsided. We stopped at the table where Frank snatched up his aluminum Rayovac flashlight, and we headed out through the back door. Now I was really puzzled.

Of course a blind man could tell by the smell that we were approaching an outside crapper. Whatever was about to unfold would manifest itself at the outhouse. Frank propped open the door and yanked me inside, while handing me the flashlight. "Hold on and don't you dare drop that flashlight." Frank had a hold on each of my ankles. The next thing I knew I was upside down and hanging above the hole. He said, "My lighter is down there. Get it."

What the heck, I obviously thought to myself. Frank lowered me down into that dark abyss. A beam of light clearly revealed this observation as my shoulders rubbed against the cutout hole. This, I determined straight away, was going to be a one-bounce dive with no second attempt. Then slightly to the side of the heaped up turds, the Rayovac beam caught the reflection of the embedded chrome Zippo cigarette lighter. I made the retrieval. "Don't worry about falling in, it'll be easier to make another one of you than clean you up," he stated. I washed my hands off and went back to bed.

The next morning Mom was up fixing breakfast. I walked past the bedroom where Frank was asleep. On the dresser laid his pocket watch with its Caterpillar watch fob, a Rayovac flashlight, and that precious Zippo cigarette lighter. And the brothers? They were preparing for another routine day at the Smith House. As I look back on it I was the most logical choice. I've got to give Frank some consideration. Gayle would have put up too much of a fight, and there was no way he was going to lift Jim, let alone get him through the hole. The choice then was skinny me.

Embedded in my memory at the Smith House, however, were many convivial evenings. For instance, on Friday night, Mom, Lois, and the boys all sat around our new Sears and Roebuck radio. We listened to the Grand Old Opry. Minnie Pearl gave us a great big old "Howdy." Roy Acuff fiddled out the Wabash Cannon Ball. Little Jimmy Dickens implored us to "Take a Cold Tater and Wait." Grandpa Jones was putting out the fire and "calling in the dogs, 'cause the hunt's over boys." We all wondered what Martha White biscuits might taste like. These were the evenings when that drafty old house caught each of our imaginations and carried them off into some distant place where we were kings and queens.

The California trip

Dogwood blossoms lingered, soon to be overpowered by the explosion of green leaves in early May, when a vehicle came down Fox Road and pulled into the driveway of our newly acquired Smith residence. It was dark blue, almost black, and on top was a luggage rack. Frank stepped out from behind the steering wheel beaming from ear to ear. He was the owner of a brand new 1952 Studebaker Champion two-door sedan. It was to my eyes the most beautiful automobile I had ever seen. Its radiance sitting there on the gravel made the Smith House and the surroundings even drearier looking. The Studebaker yanked out about seventeen hundred dollars of Frank's money from somewhere. No one, not even Mom, asked where. But we did keep asking if it was really ours. We were so enthralled with looking at the chrome bumpers, seeing our image in the chromed moon pie hubcaps, and the reverence of the immaculate interior. We gave little notice to Mom and Frank's low-toned conversation, and as we approached the door handles an unbendable command issued out of Frank's mouth: "Don't touch it!" The tone of his voice made the command very clear to us.

Everett and Aggie pulled in with their two kids. Mom and Aggie were laughing and making comments about the new car. Frank and Everett were already raising the hood of the 'Champ.' The hood came up, and we all crowded in to look at the motor. It was the first V-8 engine I ever laid eyes on. It was the most spotless mechanical device any of us had ever seen. It was a complete new Studebaker design made for the company's centennial celebration. The first Champion rolled off the line on the morning of February 8. It was one of Studebaker's 7,130,875 vehicles ever produced. Before 1952 was over Studebaker would make sixty-four thousand more Champions. I don't know what number our Champ would have been, but certainly it had to be an earlier model.

"It shines like a diamond in a goat's ass," Uncle Everett volunteered.

"Yep, zero to sixty in seventeen seconds," Frank said. "It'll get close to twenty-seven miles to the gallon, I was told," Frank continued on with his victory speech.

"About three thousand miles out there ain't it?" Everett asked more in a factual than inquisitive tone.

"Yep." Frank replied.

I asked myself, where is "out there"? All of us boys looked at each other in a quizzical way. What's in the making here? The excitement electrified the air. Everyone sensed a big adventure in the making.

Mom had been saving up a sum of money. I don't know to this day how she did it, but she did, just like I don't know how Frank swung the deal for the new car, but he did it. I guess it was all that overtime he'd been putting in. No matter, something big was coming down for sure. The new car, all the preparations Mom was making, and Frank looking over road maps told us the secret was no longer classified—we were going on a huge road trip. We were going to California.

It had been too many years since Mom had seen her brother, Fred Moorehead, who lived in Pasadena, California. Arrangements were being made to stay with Fred's family. We learned that the family had the same number of kids as ours did, except only reversed in gender. Fred had four girls and one boy, who was the youngest, and we had four boys and one girl, who was the youngest. Whatever deal was struck up between Mom and Frank has never been revealed, but the entire family was going to go.

Preparations for the oncoming great adventure were being made. Mom packed a gas pressurized cooking stove, skillets, eating utensils, and a new metal insulated ice chest. She packed each of our clothes and also packed up blankets and pillows. As we had been let in on the overall plan, we knew that we were to camp our way across America to California. Our baggage was all nicely loaded and secured by Frank on top of the car's rack. Earlier he had taken a spare tire and jack with an assortment of tools and stored them in the trunk.

Grandpa Arnold and Everett would take care of the livestock. We would be up and gone in the morning, long before the sun's rays hit the roof of the Smith House.

Frank was at the helm with Lois, Jimmie, and Vivian up front and Gayle, Ed, and me in the rear. This would be the assigned seating. Among the rear seat gang there would be a constant battle over who sat on the outside with Frank usually settling the dispute.

The Champ and its crew headed west on U.S. 50. The sun broke over the horizon and shone on the back of our necks just as we crossed the Wabash River.

Illinois farmers were out doing chores in the fields on both sides of U.S. 50. Nothing impressed me as being so unusual crossing Illinois—not a whole lot different landscape than at home. The little towns and cities were mundane farm communities.

The adventure started for me when we came into East St. Louis, passing along the massive railroad yard. Then suddenly the "Big Muddy"

Mississippi River came into view as we crossed over the Chain of Rocks Bridge into Missouri. Quickly we passed the great river, leaving behind the scene of the tug boats pushing the long line of barges. We were now on the "Great Mother Road," U.S. Route 66. As we skirted the greater St. Louis area, there were a lot of "look there, looky over there, what's that," with heads turning and bodies twisting to get a good look. We pulled into a filling station on the other side of St. Louis, and while the uniformed attendant was filling the tank, we boys sprawled out across the station's front, looking for a place to pee. And we would have done so behind a tow truck if Mom hadn't quickly stopped us. One of the first of many "hick" corrections Mom instituted. Frank was talking to the attendant about the virtues of the Champ. The dapper-dressed attendant checked the oil and then washed our windshield. The sun, when we pulled back out on Route 66, was in our eyes.

The Missouri landscape was nothing like the Indiana and Illinois farm lands—much hillier, more like mountains. I cannot say with certainty in Missouri the exact spot where Frank decided we would pitch our first bivouac shelter on this adventure. From Mom's comments I guessed it was somewhere near Jessie James's hideout. Frank's process of choosing a camping area resembled his same method for picking our houses. It was a rural area where we pulled off on a little side road and along a railroad. Someone had camped on the other side, and we discussed whether this was a possible hobo camp. Mom said, "A darn hobo wouldn't even camp here." The only pertinent thing about this camping place was it was free. We made our nature calls in the side ditch of the railroad. Frank and Gayle pitched a makeshift tent of tarps and blankets. Mom pumped up the gas stove. Orange and blue flames curled up and over the pot. We had a pleasant enough supper. Soon enough flashlight beams flickered up into the tops of surrounding trees and down the rails in both directions. Often there were night sounds that no one—not even Frank—recognized, which instantly brought forth those same yellow beams shooting out from the camp. But eventually peaceful sleep came over us, for a while anyway. We were brought straight up out of sleep by a distant roar coming our way. Tornado! No, what the heck? Then rushing air that was pushed by the speeding freight train came blasting by, sucking the tarps off our campsite as we huddled closely to save our lives. It seemed like an eternity before the train passed by.

In the morning, my eyes opened to a gray dawn and a disheveled camp site. I crawled out from under the arms and legs of Jim, Ed, and Gayle. Mom and Frank were already packing up. I took a morning pee right on the rails as I furiously slapped mosquitoes off of my neck. I heard Mom tell Frank in a very stern voice, "I'm not going to be sleeping with the scorpions and snakes anymore. From now on we stay at campgrounds."

Frank mumbled something unintelligible. We broke camp and repacked the tarps, blankets, and the stove. Breakfast wasn't being served here at Hobo Heaven; we got it later on down the road at a nice roadside table.

Some miles down the road after breakfast there was a noticeable difference in the surrounding geography. The lush green of Missouri was turning brown, and the healthy green smell gave way to an acrid rotten egg smell of sulfur and lead. We were in Galena, Kansas.

Frank interjected that 'galena' was a word that kind of meant lead. "Just like Galena, Illinois," he said, "big lead mines." In less than thirty minutes we were out of Kansas, and the crew of the Champ was crossing into Oklahoma. We traveled a good bit into "Okie" country, as Frank called it, when we approached the city limits of Tulsa. Here we made a refueling stop, and Mom did some grocery shopping. Frank stopped at a Shell station, and while an attendant was filling it up, he went inside and was talking to another man about something he was pointing at on down the road. The boys and I wandered in behind Frank, and that's when Ed punched me in the rib and pointed to the wall. There she was as beautiful as anything I had ever seen on a calendar. On a 1952 Shell calendar, a yellow two-piece clad bathing beauty towered over us, and even Frank was stealing admiring glances at her. To get a little closer to this Okie amazon, I used the pretense to "see when my birthday was going to be." On down the road Frank made a stop at a hardware store that the attendant had pointed out, and after a few minutes he came back with a water bag that carried extra water for the radiator. This canvas bag fit nicely up in front of the Champ's grill.

Cattle chutes and pens of cattle seemed to line both sides of the road into and out of Tulsa, and cowboys were everywhere you wanted to look. The 'ka shook…ka shook" swishing sounds of the oil pumps were just about as plentiful as cattle pens.

Somewhere between Tulsa and Oklahoma City, we pulled into a roadside camping and cabin site. We all stayed in a five-dollar-per-night cabin, and for twenty-five cents more we could get a radio. This was to be our mode of operation for the rest of the trip. We never stayed at the nicer places that always seemed to be across the road—the ones with fancy neon lights or the ones that you could stay in that were shaped like teepees. At the places we stayed while heading west, the cabin dwellers and camper kids could gather and play on swings and slides. Often a caravan of cars pulling campers that resembled wagon trains paraded off the road and through these same grounds.

Every once in a while, Frank would pull into some roadside attraction, the kind where you could see a two-headed rattlesnake or just an ordinary one, or where you could talk to the last Apache who fought alongside Geronimo, for example. On occasion a cold pop or some treat would come our way, but it was dang sure a slim occurrence. Our treats came at the roadside picnic tables at lunch. We would pull in and stretch ourselves out. Mom would have two of us haul the ice chest over to the table, and she would start slicing the baloney and laying it out on the white bread, which was either a bit soggy or a bit dried out. There might be a tomato sliced up on it and plenty of mayonnaise that squished out of your sandwich. Plenty of iced tea or Kool-Aid was available to wash it all down to slake our thirst.

Frank was more affable than normal on this adventure and, at this particular part of Okie country, he told us about how the big dust clouds of the thirties closed off the sun in Illinois and blanketed everything with a fine silting of dust. "All through this area, the wind picked up the topsoil and blew it off to the east—the 'Dust Bowl,' they called it." Looking out across the plains, with the wind blowing even while Frank spoke, it was easy to visualize, especially since we looked like Tom Joad's family in The Grapes of Wrath.

The Champ and its crew headed on west across windblown Okie country and into Texas, all of which meshed together as the same place. Somewhere in this area, Frank and I had a confrontation, and I owe a big part of my behind to a truck driver.

Now, the pecking order inside the Champ had pretty much been decided by the time we got down to the panhandle of Texas. Neither Frank nor Mom ever rode in the back. Sometimes Jim and Lois came back and one of us went to the front. Sometimes Mom drove, but it was usually Frank. In the back the Champs rear window made a graceful semicircle around to the front acting like side windows. This created a rather large rear dash area behind the seat, and eventually I slithered up out across the top like an old dog sunning himself. Frank never said anything, and this arrangement gave everyone in the back much more breathing room.

One time, the Champ followed in behind a semitrailer pulling a full load of something in its shining green box trailer. We tried a couple of times to get around it, but without success. Frank nosed out behind the trailer and called on the Champ for whatever it could give as we passed the matching green REO tractor. When we passed, I flashed a middle finger to the trucker. I don't know why. The heat, the boredom or just being a knucklehead, but I just gave it to him.

Frank was looking in the rear view mirror and saw it. "Did you just give that trucker a finger," he asked.

Stunned by this interrogation I immediately replied, "NO!" We broke over the rise, and in the rear I saw the trucker being left behind, end of story. Well not quite; the next time I looked back, the trucker was right on our tail, signaling that he was pulling in to the right and so were we. I looked up and the big red flying horse symbol of Mobile gas was ahead. Refuel for both. Oh no!

Frank got out, and with me, walked over to the trucker. This is it! Somewhere out here in this desolate land Tom would be buried and forgotten to history. Frank didn't beat around the tumbleweed when he asked the trucker, "Did he give you the finger?" What seemed like a lifetime passed before the trucker said "no."

I think the truck driver and Frank telegraphically understood the unfolding drama. It was obvious I was shaken, and I'm sure that both the men standing before me knew I had gotten the lesson. Thank you REO cowboy.

After these fleeting incidents of the trucker and the yellow two-piece bathing beauty slipped from my mind, we approached a sign that Mom read as the Continental Divide. As she explained how the drainage of America worked, Frank summed it up rather nicely as this: "If you stand on the line and pee on the east side it goes to the Mississippi, and if you pee on the west side it goes to the Pacific Ocean." He paused, giving us time to admire this knowledge, and then added, "We've been going uphill ever since we left St. Louis, and now from here on we're going downhill." Good enough for us.

We dropped down into Gallup, New Mexico, with a Santa Fe freight train roaring alongside. This was our first real closeup to the land of the Navaho Indian. We spent no time in Gallup; we just cruised through as the Champ protected us from the blistering sun. We were nearing Arizona and started seeing advertisements for the Grand Canyon. We traversed on through Flagstaff and never looked back. Eventually, we pulled into a camping and cabin site in Holbrook, Arizona. Across from where we would bunk up for the night was the Wigwam's Camping Grounds, with its rows of large white teepees, and we could only imagine what one might have looked like inside. At night, a light from the apex shone over the tops of them, and from our vantage point, it really looked like an Indian village. I counted at least fifteen.

Back on the road the next morning, we veered off of Route 66 and headed north to Las Vegas. More than likely both Mom and Frank might have wanted to see "the strip," but I remember going to Hoover Dam. At the dam Mom was allowed to take us on a free tour because the ticket man felt sorry for us since we were such a big crew. We descended into the inner workings of the great project, and then headed across the Mojave Desert. We had a long drive that day and into the evening. Sometime in the night, between dozing off and snapping back from sleep, we came to the Arroyo Seco Parkway—America's first freeway,
and mine, too. We reached Uncle Fred and Aunt Sadie's Pasadena home in the late hours.

The first week we acclimated ourselves with the surroundings and our host. This was the first time that any of us had been able to sit down in front of a television. I was absolutely absorbed. Every day we watched the full thirty minutes of Howdy Doody. Host Buffalo Bob Smith would ask, "Say kids, what time is it? It's Howdy Doody time." The kids in the peanut gallery would sing "It's Howdy Doody time." Clarabell the Clown would dodge from a window to a door, and then come out honking his horn or squirting his seltzer. Chief Thunderthud from the Ooragnak tribe (kangaroo spelled backwards) might appear, or Princess Summerfall Winterspring might make an appearance. But, of course, the real star of the show was Howdy himself, with his 48 freckles that represented each state. Howdy was sure to get involved in some predicament that came to a side-splitting climax.

The biggest event of our stay? We appeared on a local television program and won the grand prize: a "city dog." As far as I know they could have scooped the mutt up off of a Pasadena city alley. Now we would have eight riding together back east.

There, in front of us revealed how the rest of America would eventually roll. I remember going down the Arroyo Seco Parkway, which was the first interstate highway, the one that became the first leg of Route 66. As we came over a rise, as far as you could see, there were houses being built. There was a "get a move on and get out of the way" mindset. Everything seemed frenzied.

An unpleasant event for Ed and Lois was when they explored a hillside behind Uncle Fred's house, and they both received a severe case of poison oak. For the longest time they could have passed for lepers.

I don't recall if Mom toured Hollywood; I can't imagine her missing that because it was just a few miles away from Fred's place. I also don't remember seeing the Pacific Ocean because we wouldn't have skipped seeing that either. All of the Los Angeles area came together like the Okie and Texas plains to me; where it started or stopped, I couldn't say.

During our trip, Frank changed the oil, and since the Champ was showing too much grime, he also had it washed so it shined again like that goat's diamond. Shortly after, we visited a Dairy Queen, where we were all treated to an ice cream cone. The windows were down, and the California sun was melting my ice cream pretty fast. I didn't want to stain the cleaned interior, so I stuck my head out of the window, and, of course, the wind slathered the drippings all over the side of the Champ. Frank gave me a good verbal chewing, but that's as far as it went. Sometimes any decision you make is the wrong one.

For the time we stayed it was amusing enough, until "a skunk came to the picnic" when Frank and Fred had a disagreement, and Frank gave the orders to "pack immediately, we were leaving." And we did.

We said our goodbyes, and the crew of the Champ with one little squirmy mutt went blazing back through the San Bernardino Mountains to catch Route 66 with the sun in our faces.

Frank must have felt like he needed to make up for the brisk departure because we traveled south to the Guadalupe Mountains to tour Carlsbad Caverns, then we split New Mexico in half driving north to Pikes Peak. The Champ and all eight of us ascended to the top with Mom admonishing Frank for being so close to the edge the entire 14,110 feet. We were up there just long enough to get altitude sickness, and then we came back down to start working our way back to Indiana. I don't recall any particular event going back, with one exception. When we hit the greenery of Missouri, the humidity of June slapped us back to reality. We had left the West behind.

CHAPTER FIVE

Hoosier Land

After we got back home from California, it took about a week for us to push back the growth from around the Smith House. Our routines picked up right where we left them, and the good old Studebaker Champion was decommissioned by Frank. He traded or sold the sedan for an older model truck, but a decent one. And while the "Champ" would be missed, it was understood as a practical move. The truck had tool boxes on it—Frank picked up a few ideas out there on the coast.

At this time the baby boom and Korean conflict increased a demand for energy, and Frank and Everett were working full time at the strip mines. The Korean War ignited an economic boom, but it also ushered in the "Red Scare" and the stalemate of the war. The war was being called a "police action," frustrating everyone in my sphere. The ten-year-old me felt a sense that people thought it was time for a new approach in America.

By mid-summer 1952, everywhere you looked there were "I LIKE IKE" buttons, signs, and political conversations. Grandpa Arnold, a Republican precinct committee man, drove a flatbed in parades with red, white, and blue bunting wrapped along the side and a two-sided sign emblazed with the words "VOTE FOR IKE." Throughout the county he patrolled with a speaker mounted on the truck, extolling the virtues of Ike. I often rode on the back and tossed out candy in the parades. It looked like our next president would be Dwight D. Eisenhower; anyway, that was the hope of my family. It wasn't at all clear how it would affect us.

The summer carried on as well as to be expected. I picked up the usual hay-making jobs and still had plenty of time to go swimming in the pits with my buddies. There were other times at the strip mines that I spent with Frank. I'd sit for hours on end, watching as he operated an old Bucyrus-Erie dragline. I watched Frank operate the "sticks" and pedals that sent the boom slinging out the hoist cables and dropping the dragline bucket. With a pull or push of a lever, the drag cable would start winding in. The drag chains rattled and clinked as the dragline bucket filled up. And then, with the movement of a surgeon—"a dirt surgeon"—Frank would push a pedal and pull a lever, and the cab and boom would move ever so gracefully and sling over the spoil pile, releasing the drag cable and slackening hoist chains on the bucket. The overburden toppled down on the peak of the pile. Over the pit the boom would swing with a taut hoist cable being released at the precise moment and with perfect placement of the bucket every single time. Frank was darn good.

He performed this over and over, stopping only to grease the turntable or swing the cab out over the edge and off the high wall to relieve himself from the cabin's doorway or for lunch break. Camel cigarette smoke laced with the smell of shale, grease, and diesel fumes infiltrated the air all during the shift.

The draglines in these smaller strip mine operations were usually large enough to pull a forty to fifty-foot high wall, enough to get the easy top vain of coal. To help the dragline move the overburden, Uncle Everett would operate a bulldozer, creating a level bench for the dragline to set on while pushing overburden to the dragline bucket. I sat on the side of the seat with Uncle Everett hours at a time, and often he would turn the dozer over to me to get the "feel." The power of earth moving machinery being controlled through the manipulation of levers and pedals from my hands and feet gave me an enormous amount of self-confidence. This was something I could do, something I recognized as being an important skill set where I could find my future purpose. It was a language that I quickly learned to communicate. It was a book I could read.

It often fell to Everett to drill and load holes for the demolition of the overburden, and it was on one of these occasions that I was with him when he loaded the holes with dynamite. He tied in the fuse and set a match to it. We jumped in the truck and headed up the ramp out of the pit to find cover before the blast. KA-Boom! Whoosh!

The blast went off on us halfway up the ramp. Fallout from the blast fell all around us and on the truck—boulders, it seemed to me. I was slightly shaken, but Uncle Everett didn't break his stride at all. He drove through the blast dust and over to where the pit boss was coming out from his protection. Everett asked, "How much does this fuse cost per foot?"

The pit boss said, "Five cents a foot."

Everett reached inside of his pocket and pulled out fifty cents, then handed the pit boss the change and said with a straight-face (which was incredible for someone who just darn near got blown to bits) "next time buy ten more feet."

The rest of the summer of '52 melted away like that California ice cream cone. When, all of the sudden it seemed, we Harrawood boys, with our sister Lois, were standing out at the end of the driveway huddled together. By our demeanor you'd think we were headed for an orphanage, but really we were just waiting for our first bus ride to school; not to Cannelburg, but to Montgomery, Indiana.

Our school bus for the next two years was on a GMC chassis with a Carpenter body. Our bus, a yellow "Kid Hack" as Ralph Carpenter called it, came off the Carpenter assembly line about forty miles east in Mitchell, Indiana. There was an assortment of busses lined up at Montgomery

School. It was possible to see a Ford, a Dodge, a Studebaker, an International Harvester, or a Chevrolet/GMC. All of them had, however, a Carpenter body attached.

Montgomery was founded in 1865 by Valentine Montgomery. It was a spot to ship and receive from the Ohio and Mississippi railway, later to become the Baltimore and Ohio railway. Montgomery's population in the 1950s wasn't much over 550 souls. Geographically about the only other significance was that it was the halfway point on the railroad between Cincinnati and St. Louis, and it was, at 528 feet, the highest elevation on the railroad between these two cities. The economy was mostly agriculture-based. The town supported the grain mill that we watched our free movies on, as well as an Allis Chalmers dealer, a welding shop, a grocery store, a post office, a bank, two bars, and two gas stations. The town was built around a large Catholic church. St. Peter's steeple could be seen for a long distant away, the second oldest Catholic parish in Indiana.

During the first school year at Montgomery, it didn't take long for me to learn my way around. There were plenty of acquaintances that I knew from the free movies, and others I had met at different community functions. Nicknames like Snake, Tater, Willie, Freak, and Popper all became my posse for the rest of my Montgomery school days.

The fourth grade was organized in the same alphabetical seating order that I was familiar with, just as the classroom and desks were all familiar. The fourth grade was purely a continuation of my third: a hodgepodge of cheating, clowning, shrewdness, and buffoonery. All of this was to escape reading or oral presentations, which was a veneer covering a boy who really wanted to learn, but was too far in the hole, academically.

Thanksgiving was again at my grandparent's farm. Then Christmas came and we celebrated at the Smith House. Santa came and left a few goodies, but unlike the new hit song, I never "Saw Mommy Kissing Santa

Claus." For the rest of the school break I was busy carting out the chamber pots, doing the milking, and hauling in lumps of coal. On New Year's Eve, while Frank and Mom were out and about celebrating, we kids sat around and ate ham sandwiches and big bowls full of Mom's red beans and dumplings, and of course, soda pop. While on our radio, Hiram King Williams, everyone knew him as "Hank," mournfully sang his most recent hit, "Your Cheatin' Heart." The next day, on the first day of January 1953, we heard on the local radio station that Hank had died earlier in the morning.

Mr. Eisenhower was inaugurated as the president. To celebrate this Mom treated us to a movie at the Indiana Theater in Washington, Indiana, to watch Grace Kelly and Gary Cooper in High Noon. I finished the rest of my fourth-grade school year, and I had no high noon shootout with the teachers. I surmised that they would just as soon let the next grade deal with me; after all, it was certainly no benefit to my teacher to keep me around another year. And so the Tommy tin can was kicked on up to the fifth grade.

The summer of '53 changed the culture at the Smith House, thanks to the purchase of our Admiral television. The summer heat was too intense and stifling to sit and watch inside the Smith House, so Frank placed it facing outwards in a window. We would take chairs or sit on blankets and watch from outside. A big bowl of popped corn saturated with lard grease and then salted down, with slabs of Old Betsy's butter melting over the top, followed with Mom's ice tea, made for a most pleasant evening of TV watching, even with the persistent slaps in the audience from the mosquito bites. TV, from an early age on, substituted for books, opening up for me a world that I could never discover in the written word.

No new intellectual discoveries enlightened me in the fifth grade. The only difference in this school year was that I had my first encounter with a male teacher: Mr. Frank.

Indiana in the 1950s still maintained a single class basketball tournament. The rural Indiana landscape was still doggedly holding on to their little schools. Their basketball teams could once in a while win local tournaments, or even their sectional. To advance much further and win a regional was an exceptional accomplishment.

Montgomery did go to the Indiana Sweet Sixteen in 1935, and they won a sectional in 1952, losing against Jasper in the final game of the regional. But it was the only time, and they never won another while I was there at Montgomery. One exception was a holiday tournament in the 1955-56 season that my brother Gayle played in. The basketball-crazed town of Montgomery and the entire Hoosier state was in an uproar over a little school named Milan.

The Milan Indians had only two losses in the regular season. The Indians achieved victory in their sectional, went on to win their regional, and then on to the semi-state tournament. Milan had twice the enrollment of their next competitor, the Montezuma's Aztecs. The Aztec Tribe, with all of their students including the team, totaled seventy-nine. The Milan Indians conquered the Aztecs. And in the next game against Crispus Attucks with the future Hall of Fame player, Oscar Roberts, Milan came out as the winner and was now headed for the state championship.

The state championship heavily favored five-time state champs, the Muncie Central Bearcats. After three quarters Bobby Plump, the Indian's star shooter, shot poorly—only two for ten from the field. Bobby froze the ball and held it for over four minutes during the waning fourth quarter. Tied at 30 … the clock ticked away the seconds, Bobby Plump, as cool as a cucumber, … eight, seven, six, five, four, three … Bobby shot and hit a 14-footer from the right side as the buzzer went off. The state of Indiana roared!

Milan had a population of twelve hundred, but as the story has been told, for thirteen miles out of town over forty thousand celebrating Hoosiers stood on both sides of the road cheering the returning Indians. It would be for all time that every Hoosier kid with a basketball would put himself in the shoes of Bobby Plump and reenact that scene over and over. My Brother Ed was one of them. From that time on, he was hardly seen without a basketball.

There was another champion that spring in fifth grade class. How else would you describe a boy who never once did homework or was ever seen clutching a book be passed on to the sixth grade?

To Make the Best Better

The summer began with the normal Smith House operations: a garden was created and odd jobs were being sought by us boys. Farmers hired me to help with planting, but mostly I filled the planter and the fertilizer boxes. Sometimes I would even have the opportunity to pull a disc or harrow behind a tractor, but planting—that was way too important to be in my hands. Generally, I only advanced the truck along with the planter with bags of fertilizer and seed corn. Once I was working for a farmer doing exactly that. I needed to back up his recently purchased pickup, and because I was too short to see in the mirror, I opened the door and was leaning out to see when I hit a stump in the fence row and jammed the door. "D#$*!" I was trying to fix it while the farmer was making a round, but there was no fixing it. Every time you opened or closed the door it made a "kerklunk…kerklunk" sound and dipped slightly about half way out or in. He wasn't very happy about that, but as far as I was concerned he had it coming. I had to get up one day at two a.m. and go to Louisville, Kentucky, with the old tight wad to load fertilizer bags—hundred pounders each. He distributed them to other farmers. I unloaded and stacked them by myself all day. At the end of the day, he asked me how much I wanted to be paid. I was reasonable enough and said three dollars. He said, "Too much, "I'll pay you two." I didn't need a book to learn how to price my labor the next time.

Summer days during the rest of my grade school adventures were broken up by our regular 4-H meetings. Our chapter was called the "East Barr Boys." The meetings were hosted by Mom on occasion at the Smith House, and we would have many of the members attend. The organization's purpose was to take the rural youth, ages nine to nineteen, and enhance their education in agriculture, home economics, and the development of good citizenship. The name came from the four-leaf clover, with each leaf representing an H for: Head, Hands, Heart, and Health.

The club pledge: "I pledge my Head to clearer thinking, my Heart to greater loyalty, my Hands to larger service, and my Health for better living for my Club, my Community, and my Country." That was the first order of business. Then we would also in unison say the club motto: "To Make the Best Better." Of course we started our meeting with The Pledge Of Allegiance.

"To Make the Best Better," in Mom's view was what she wished for her sons and the community. 4-H chapters were organized in many of the townships, but few were organized and directed by a woman. Mom was an early (if not the first) female 4-H volunteer sponsor in the county, most certainly of the East Barr Boys. She really did a wonderful job. We had special guests who gave talks to our chapter on various subject. One special appearance at an East Barr Boys meeting was "Uncle Bob Harding," a local TV celebrity from WTTV out of Bloomington, about fifty-plus miles north, whom we faithfully watched. His show was called "The Western Ledger," and he entertained with songs and stories before he introduced a western movie. His co-star was his horse named "Rhythm." Uncle Bob also had a traveling show called the "Hayloft Frolic." He brought it to the gym in Montgomery, costing us kids thirty-five cents to get in. Better than that, Uncle Bob came by himself to the East Barr Boys 4-H meeting held at the All Saints Catholic Church hall in Cannelburg. We all gathered around him, and he sang songs and told stories, all thanks to Mom.

On other occasions the clubs came together for our Wednesday night softball games. These were just absolutely the best times—good-natured competition usually ending with a cookout. The games would always have fans making them even more exciting. My best buddy and 4-H partner was Gary Love.

On a hot and humid summer day, my good buddy Gary Love and I were putting hay up for a farmer when his nose started bleeding. We did all sorts of things to try and stop it. Brother Ed suggested placing a quarter under his tongue. I'm not sure where that quarter or that remedy came from, but I'll bet it wasn't Ed's. Odds are, though, Ed ended up with the quarter. We finally got Gary's bleeding stopped, and he went home. This was the prelude to the death of my dear friend. This sort of bleeding thing continued with him. His folks, with nearly enough kids to have two softball teams, didn't just run to the doctor every time one bleeds. But it became patently obvious there was something wrong with Gary. He was admitted to the hospital. We all suspected something was deadly serious because Gary would have never missed a big Wednesday 4-H game. We all knew how much it meant to him.

For as long as Gary was in the hospital, I hitchhiked over to Washington and visited him. He fell deeply in love with a nurse's aide, and for that I was happy. One night as his mother and I were walking out of his room, he called for his mother, and then he died.

I was one of those who carried his coffin to the grave. As we came out of the church with him, we walked through a gauntlet of his classmates; girls lined on one side and boys on the other. It was a sad day for all. Gary was taken down by leukemia.

Besides being a sponsor for 4H, Mom was a member of the Indiana Home Demonstration Chorus. This was a Purdue University program that helped 4-H clubs put on plays and concerts as well as to help promote the arts for rural families. It also sponsored community concerts.

A big event for this organization was scheduled for August of 1954. Out of ninety-two counties in Indiana, one thousand representatives from eighty-eight of the counties were going to Los Angeles to perform at the Hollywood Bowl for a performance to benefit the Children's Hospital of Los Angeles. The event was estimated to draw up to twenty-two thousand spectators and was to be broadcast by radio and television across the nation.

Governor Knight of California declared the entire state of California on August 22 as "Indiana Day." It was a really big deal, drawing lots of press attention. There was one little catch, though—you had to pay for your own transportation out and back, plus other expenses.

Mom realized that Frank wouldn't be able to afford this trip for her. She was very depressed, but practical, and told the leader of the chorus it simply was not economically feasible. Well, one little bird told another. The word went all the way up to the top director of Home Demonstrations at Purdue University, who was connected to the producer of a popular show of the time based in Chicago, Illinois, called "Welcome Travelers."

Mom discussed this with her Daviess County Chorus Director, who, along with other members, encouraged her to write to Tommy Bartlett, the star of the "Welcome Travelers" TV shows about the chorus and the benefit. Mr. Bartlett invited her to appear. Mom was led to understand that the interview would be about the Home Demonstrators Chorus and the Los Angeles benefit for children. The interview was, to Mom's amazement, about how she had 'overcome her objections to having a large family and found unlimited joy and satisfaction in her family of four boys and one girl.'

Mom was so bewildered by the hustle of getting a TV show on the air that she didn't know what to do about it without being impolite. The TV interview was aired at the Children's Hospital and on the Los Angeles TV and radio stations across more than five states; moreover, it was broadcast to the student body of Purdue, University, several more stations across Indiana, and the entire Chicago viewing area. The Mayor of Los Angeles had a special luncheon to view the show.

To say the least, our mother was greatly embarrassed that it only dealt with her plight in life. "Welcome Travelers" ran from 1952 thru 1955, and it was up against the other same big time slots on TV, including "The Garry Moore Show," "American Bandstand," and the first super reality show, "Queen for a Day."

"Queen for a Day" was so popular at the time that it was picking up a cool $4,000 per minute in advertisement. Tommy Bartlett's "Welcome Travelers" in Chicago was trying to mirror the style of "Queen for a Day." Mom appeared exactly at this time and became an ersatz "Queen for a Day." Her humiliation was appeased somewhat because she won a set of tires with tubes, a new automatic washer, a portable automatic record player, an electric blanket, a hair dryer, and also dinner in a fine Chicago restaurant. For all the rest of our days the story would be that she was "a queen for a day." When she returned with all her riches, she also had in her possession another city mutt. Who knows how Mom obtained the registered cocker spaniel, but we assumed it was one of her prizes. This red-and-cinnamon-speckled dog was with her when she returned to the Smith House.

No one remembers what happened to our Pasadena mutt. Someone said they last saw it out in the pig lot. It didn't seem to us to be a coincidence that the top hit on the charts when the new dog (who took the name Pepper) moved in was "Doggie in the Window." Mom thought that she could make a buck or two by breeding Pepper and selling her pups. Before long we had little squirmy "Peppers" in a cardboard box.

Frank, the "professional dog man," was going to bob the tails on the little Peppers, when Mom wondered aloud if that would hurt them. Frank said that it would not because he'd "only cut off small parts at a time."

This was the time that we learned we would soon be living in a new home—our very own—on the five acres that Frank bought from Grandpa Arnold. From the Smith House the property, as the crow flies, was a little over a mile due west, on what was known as the Corning Road. By roadway it was about two miles. We may have had grandiose ideas of what the new home would look like, but in the end Frank wouldn't disappoint us.

He rented or traded labor with a nearby contractor who had a small dragline. With this he made a clean cellar cut, (this being the basement foundation of the future home) piling the dirt over to the side just like the spoil piles in the strip mines. Jim and I were told not to play on the pile. "Okay." But he caught us on it anyway, giving us a good chewing out and sending us walking back home. Now, if we were crows we could have flown straight home. But we didn't have feathers, so the two bare-footed boys headed south one half mile, then east one mile, then north one-half mile, all on gravel. Before too long our feet, tough as they were, started to hurt, with small lacerations and bruises. So, we loosened up our pants and slipped the pant legs down over our feet and began walking backward.

Frank did his best to have our new home ready for us to move into before the school year started. I do not recall any celebration about moving "down" into our new home. We made our last move into our last Indiana home, and I was headed into the final years of grade school.

Back Words

CHAPTER SIX

The Basement House

It was quite literally a block house in the ground with a flat roof that had some sort of screening to help adhere the black tar substance on the top. The boys at the D-Day landing would have recognized it right off with its ground-level basement windows, about one foot tall and two feet wide, perfect for machine guns. The freshly graded bare clay around it made it look even more like an enemy bunker.

A flight of poured concrete stairs, about twelve steps, led down into this subterranean dwelling. There was light, but only narrow shafts of it coming in from the gun ports; otherwise, it was as "dark as a coal mine." Its interior, or what you could adjust your eyes to see, was made of raw concrete blocks that needed paint. This hollow chamber had no interior walls, and the so-called "walls" we ended up with were curtains. There was what seemed to be something that resembled a bathroom, but for now we washed outside in galvanized wash tubs. Instead of going downstairs to the outhouse, we now had to go upstairs. Drainage pipes were established for the kitchen, and an eventual bathroom, but there was no running water, and it wouldn't be for about a year until the "Queen" finally forced Frank to hook up her washer. We eventually had central air. Frank rigged up a table fan that was suspended from the ceiling by black tape and a frayed electrical cord. It circulated something that felt like air. The only thing missing was a periscope.

But by gosh it was ours! And Frank, I guess, had a visceral sense of accomplishment with his architectural creation of this vault we called the Basement House. Frank even went so far as to landscape it. He bought a Japanese red maple and planted it out front where it still grows.

    Outside on the west and south side, the land sloped down to a creek known as Prairie South Fork. It cut a ditch to the north and west where it fishhooked up to Prairie North Fork, then wrapped around west of Washington and emptied into the West Fork of the White River. Just to the south was the head of the creek. This creek provided lots of hours of entertainment. We trapped muskrats, skinned them out, and then used them as puppets. Little oxbows in the creek created deep holes big enough to dunk ourselves completely under water. Sand and gravel bars made nice beaches. To the south of us on the east side of the road, about two tenths of a mile, was a little country church named Mt. Olive. A little past that and up on the eastern hilltop was a graveyard with tall old cedar trees. Just past the graveyard, Corning Road crossed old Hwy 50 that ran east and west.

To the north the Basement House was Grandpa Arnold and Grandma Elsie Harrawood's homestead. A little farther up the road was the Ed Scott farm. Here I would spend many an hour working for Ed and many a night sleeping in a side room. I toiled for scores of men, but it was here at the Scott farm that I learned how a kind, honest, gentle, and self-confident man was supposed to act. Ed had these attributes and many more. I cannot say enough about the decency of this man. From Ed's house the road shot straight north where it T'd at U.S. Route 50, and if you made a right and went a mile there was Four Points. If you made a left about a mile there was Montgomery. This would be my portal to the outside world; this little, muddy, buggy road led to the black asphalt paved highway For the rest of my days in Indiana, this was my exit out.

Shortly after we moved into the Basement House, I started back to school. Our new bus driver was a fellow we called "Brownie." Brownie was short and rotund who had a smile like a fox and a laugh like a snake. He was a character and made "extra" with his bus by chartering it out for school trips, 4-H outings, and basketball games. As I remember, it was anywhere from a dime to a quarter to ride on his bus, but normal school bus days were free. I thought we should have been paid by him because more than once we boys had to get out and help push the bus out of a mud hole, or through a snow drift.

While in the sixth grade, brother Jim and my good buddy Popper pulled off a small terrorist act on our teacher, Mr. Frank. They positioned a nail in such a way that Mr. Frank would puncture his tire when he left the school. Well yes, he did have a flat tire, but it was a very slow flat, and it happened at his home so only he could have known. So when he came in the next morning that clever brother of mine asked if he had a flat tire! Jim was ushered into the school office for cross examination. He finally broke down from the interrogation and admitted that he was the culprit, but not before he gave up our comrade, Popper. Both of them, for the next thirty noon-hour recesses, had to hand pump up a truck tire on the stage of the gymnasium. When the tire was full, the air was let out, and they did it over and over, again and again and again.

This kind of chicanery among my rebel friends lasted on through the sixth grade and throughout the rest of my school days. We had an immeasurable number of tactics to get us out of school. We used funerals, "good old Joe was such a family friend," for example. Another time, at Christmas, we were assigned to cut a tree for the classroom, (it never occurred to me that this created a respite for the teachers). Just when the buses started to line up to take us all home, we would trod in with the tree.

I played hard, but I also worked hard, often working immediately after school. I started working for Ed Scott from the time we moved from the Smith House to our "Basement Sweet Basement." Ed's property started across the road, and one time he hired me to put in the fence posts for a new fence line. I was paid a dime for each post I planted. I worked during the night using a lantern for light. My posts were plum bobbed straight and tamped as tight as could be. The next day Ed said "Tom you did a good job, but the post are on the wrong side of the line. You have to take them out and put them on my side of the line." Well, of course he wasn't going to pay me twice. I didn't need a book to learn this lesson: Make sure you get it right the first time!

Ed Scott never sold his farm while I was there, but he took a night job at a ball bearing plant in Washington. Several nights I stayed over because his wife had a new baby, and he felt that I would offer security. Both in the morning and evening I did his livestock feeding and whatever else needed to be done.

It wasn't just the schools that were consolidating. Families who owned a hundred acres could still barely make the bank payments, and more and more were selling out or leasing to the bigger operators. There were still plenty of days left where in the distance you could hear the squeals of hogs and the clanging of galvanized hog feeder doors being lifted and dropped by hog noses. There were still black turkeys in the hundreds being raised in the open. These open-range turkey fields provided more opportunity for employment for us boys. We were "paid assassins" who would take our rifles and set up at night to pick off roving killer dogs. (We always made sure that our dogs were tied up back at home.) Then there was the job of shooing turkeys into a corral of sorts, catching them by hand and loading the flapping sixty-pound "Toms" in cages. This was always done after school in the evening, and late into the night.

These were the days that sociologists called the "fifties doldrums," but I remember no despair. These were changing times to be sure, but there were plenty of opportunities for someone like me to make money and still have a good time. However, Frank might have agreed with the sociologists that he was definitely being hampered by those old "doldrums."

Give me that old time religion

Frank would have these sudden "come to Jesus moments." He'd sober himself up, swear off the drinking, and turn our heads south to the Mt. Olive church. Well, it was just down the road and it was hard not to take church seriously, especially if it was where your grandparents attended. When Frank thought he was "saved" enough to go back to drinking, he wouldn't bother any longer with his church attendance but still insisted that we all go.

It was a profitable experience, on every cold Sunday morning for me anyway. I was paid twenty-five cents to fire up the two potbelly coal burning stoves that set at opposite sides of the church. On the back side of the church there was a coal shed and a pile of corncobs with a jug of kerosene. I loaded up the stoves with the cobs and a lump or two of coal in each, then poured a generous amount of kerosene over the stack, struck a match, and backed off. I swear, you could see those stoves swell up before your eyes. With an enormous "WUFF," a ball of combustion would be forced up and out the chimneys making them rattle. Smoke and flames would escape from around the doors and the pipe joints. When Tom builds a fire, it's a fire! Before very long those stoves became cherry red, and it would get so hot in the church that windows were opened to cool down the building.

The old church would heat up on its own when a revival was held at Mt. Olive. I remember this preacher just out of the seminary, with his young, pretty wife. Ed and I would help them tack up revival announcements on poles and buildings for the event, and they would buy us hamburgers, fries, and milkshakes. I really came to like those folks. One evening he preached a good scorching sermon, and a call to the altar was made. No one in the benches felt the spirit enough to be committed. My friend Tommy and I felt bad for the preacher so we just got up and marched right up there to the front with everyone saying "Praise the Lord" and "Amen." The young preacher said his best for our salvation, but since we didn't have a baptismal tank, we would have to go to another church in Washington to have a real dunking.

It was a walk down in and back up out of the tank. A curtain shielded the baptized person as they walked out of what I called the "dipping tank." We were to wear a white shirt, for "holiness." I was to be the first. The preacher placed a white handkerchief over my nose and mouth as I held onto him. Up and out of the water came a saint. As I was dripping wet and walking in behind the curtain, I took my wet hanky and towel-snapped the back of Tommy's head as he was getting ready for his dip. He let out a yelp and cried "JESUS," shaking the curtain, which made it seem like it might come crashing down. Regrettably, his Daddy and mine sat right up front by the dipping tank. After the celebration of the new "saints," they asked what the commotion was all about. Frank, as usual, eventually broke me down, and I told him what I had done. Well... I had the "holy" crap whipped out of me.

When it came to being a good fighter, Frank got it, honestly. I witnessed this up close one Sunday in the bell tower lobby. It began on a party line when Grandma Elsie "just happened" to pick up the phone. She heard a conversation about her daughter, my Aunt Laura, who was...well...a woman, ah... let's just say of lesser virtues. Grandma steamed on this for a whole week, and I suppose if we had been paying closer attention we might have noticed the Cherokee blood flushing up in Grandma's cheeks,

Chapter 6 - The Basment House

but we didn't. Anyway, I really doubt anyone could have prevented what happened next.

The church bell tower was above the double door entrance. It affords a little lobby space where, after services, the congregants tend to linger a bit before stepping outside. It was at this very spot where Grandma Elsie's adversary slipped in beside her. Elsie twirled around and gave that fellow Christian a roundhouse punch while screaming a Cherokee war cry, admonishing her by saying, "You witch, don't you be calling my daughter a whore."

The rather large busybody she had just coldcocked fell backward and hit the wall. She slid down to the floor as her dress rolled up over her humongous hips. Her legs bent up and spread out exposing the most horrendous scene that is, to this day, seared in my memory. Her flesh-colored stockings were rolled down just below her knees, and her underwear reminded me of a Japanese wrestler.

Evidently, Grandma did not believe in a one-punch knockout because she commenced to kick the busybody with one foot and then another. This "Holy Toledo!" brawl took Grandpa, Frank, Mom, and the preacher everything they collectively had to pry the two women apart. Grandma was going for the kill.

That Sunday at my grandparent's house a big family intervention took place with Grandpa Arnold, Frank, and Everett trying to calm Grandma down. They pleaded with her not to return to the evening services, but by gosh nothing stops Grandma Elsie. She returned that evening and sat there just like a smoldering Vesuvius.

As you probably surmised so far, I didn't spend a whole lot of time in church, but there was one other incident that sticks out in my mind. One Sunday during service I was sitting in a pew by the window using my arm to prop the window open. In a pew behind me was Ed, who was trying to pull the window down on my arm. There was a struggle but I prevailed, pushing the window up and then resting my arm on the sill. When Ed gave a little shove to the window, it fell like a French guillotine. The window caught the skin of my upper arm and gave me a smart pinch. I pulled my arm away, which let the window come down on my fingers. I let out a yelp. I was trying to act saint-like when the congregation turned to see what happened. Oh nothing folks just my fingers sticking out of the window. Ed and I both got our Francis Earl Harrawood-style blessing back at home.

    Visiting the church graveyard seemed to have an eerie seduction for us. It was always enticing when a fresh grave was dug. Usually it was dug the day before its occupant would move in. Now, you couldn't be caught playing there in the daylight, so we would fetch our kerosene lantern and go visit the excavation after sunset. Ed, Jim, and I would stand at the edge and contemplate the ethereal things of a freshly dug grave. Once Jim and I shoved Ed in the hole. I wouldn't venture to guess what voices or visions were in his head, but you've not seen a soul claw itself up and out of a hole like Ed did. He flew past us like a ghost was on his tail. You could hear his steps hit the gravel every ten feet, all the way down the lane and back up to the house. Soon, I would be a witness to Death's shadow crossing this graveyard.

    Grandpa knew how to train crows, and he had one that we all called "Jim." Jim Crow was just one of the neatest critters you could ever be around. He liked taking things out of your hand, like a cracker. If something was missing, say a ring or a key, the first place you would look was in Jim's hooch. Jim would fly above you like a dog walking beside you. He'd go from tree to tree or pole to pole, wait for you, and then fly to the next perch. I wanted a crow. So Grandpa taught me how to train one and told me the best time to capture a crow. It just so happened that the time was right, and it just so happened that there were crows' nests in the top of those big cedars at the cemetery. Anyone who knows anything about eastern red cedar, knows that they are a tight-branched tree. That makes it hard to climb the limbs, but I was vigilant to the cause and persevered all the way to the top. I'll be the first to tell you, it was right shaky up there, but there it was, a big beautiful crow's nest, and it was full of little "Jims."

I ignored the persistent cawing of the crows while making my way up the tree. When I got the little fledgling in my hand, it became quite difficult to climb back down while maintaining a grip on my crow. Moreover, the whole murder of crows was now diving down on my head from all angles. Still, I maintained my composure, but this one particular crow and this one impossible limb created a bad combination. The fiend came in to peck at my head while the faulty limb snapped. I was grabbing at everything as I fell through the limbs and hit the ground with a thud, knocking out my breath. But, I was still breathing. Not so for my little Jim. His eyes were bulging, and his little yellow tongue hung out from the side of his twisted beak. I scuffed out a little hole with my shoe and buried him right there under his former home, that big old red cedar.

UFOs and Piper Cubs

I had so many opportunities to make money that I spent more time skipping school than attending. During the spring of 1956 I was working for local farmers as a plowboy. I should have been in school, but I was too busy making cash. It was one cool evening in a lonely field that I experienced the extraterrestrial.

Encouraged by veteran groups for the GI Bill Of Rights, FDR signed into law the Servicemen's Readjustment Act in 1944. The Veterans Bill would be known simply as the "GI Bill." It was a catalyst for the future baby boom, the expanding housing market, college enrollment, vocational schools, and in general, the post-war economic boom. Over one million GIs enrolled in college and made up half of the students who were enrolled in 1946. By 1956 over 10 million veteran men and women were attending college or vocational institutions. The GI Bill also included tuition for flying lessons so a veteran could acquire a pilot's license. The local airport sensed an opportunity. Through word of mouth and the local urging of Legionaries, it wasn't long before the sky was full of buzzing airplanes.

Veterans—down from the adrenaline rush of mortal combat—found a release in riding motorcycles and flying planes. Motorcycles were being bobbed, fenders removed, and whatever else needed to be done for more speed and power. This "need for adrenaline" was happening all over the nation. WWII cowboys who came home increased rodeo attendance, where they rode broncos and bulls. Uncle Everett, while not a cowboy, rode Harley Davidson and Indian cycles.

But, flying planes! Frank, Everett Harrawood, and a good many others were not college bound. So when word spread that the ten-year limit to use the G.I. Bill was nearing an end for WW II veterans, Frank and Everett started flying lessons. Another incentive beyond learning to fly was the money paid toward living expenses. Flying was so popular that it was typical to see a Cessna Piper Cub lazily buzzing over our heads.

"Flying Farmers" is what the Daviess County airport flyers were known as. They displayed their abilities during festival "Airport Days." The community would come out to the grass-patch airport for a show. Airplane rides were offered, which consisted mostly of a takeoff, a trip around the air strip, and a quick landing. The National Guard had their displays, with combat equipment concessions and other booths that offered various information. The real thrill for me was the formation flights that the

Flying Farmers performed. There were no serious aerobatics, just a decent display of formations, both vertical and horizontal, with a mass flyover. I was there in the crowd when a formation appeared with Frank flying one of the planes. This flight formation is a well-executed maneuver where planes fly over "stacked" at different altitudes. I swelled with pride when I overheard a woman say "oh how beautiful that is." It may well have been one of the few times that Frank was not drinking his Old Crow whiskey.

I could operate any tractor out in the fields. On one particular day, I was on a burnt-orange-colored Allis-Chalmers tractor, a WD 45, with a wide front end pulling a three-bottom plow. I skipped school that morning and went straight to the 45, checked the fuel and oil, and began plowing. I was plowing a field which bordered highway U.S. 50, when a school bus stopped to pick up some kids from across the road. Traffic stopped both ways, and behind the stopped bus was the principal of my school. We made eye contact, and I waved to him. I am certain that he understood that I was performing my life's calling.

I made the turn, dropped into the furrow, and lowered the plow into the Hoosier soil. I would repeat this maneuver until lunch time. It was customary for the farmer to provide lunch, but depending on the farmer and what he offered, I would carry some extra rations. I had a supper brought to me that particular day because I was plowing well into the dark of night.

These were the days of Eisenhower's "Atoms for Peace," fueling inspiration for stories of unidentified flying objects, UFOs, made even scarier by sci-fi movies. Movies of teenage wolfmen, giant lizards, and Martian invasions were standard for the time. When it turned dark and I was still plowing to the end of the field, a darkened tree line hastened me to make a turn. I always turned quickly while hunkering my head down into my shoulders. I pulled back hard on the throttle and watched the sparks fly out of the exhaust stack to get away as quickly as I could from that ominous tree line, where I was sure a lagoon monster lurked.

On one of those turns I felt reasonably safe from the dark boundary and had started to relax, when I noticed a light in the distance, way up in the sky. It seemed to be headed my way. By gosh, it was headed my way, straight at me. Then the light disappeared. I knew without a doubt that it was a UFO and that I was going to be abducted. After all, it was the perfect place for Martians to do their sinister work. Suddenly, a beam of light flashed outward and down on me from the spacecraft. I could not hear over the tractor engine the sound of the flying saucer that was about to snatch me away, or worse. I heard my blood curdling scream, though, as I was blinded by the light. Just as I was about to bail off the tractor, the lights of the craft came back on, and the Piper swooped up over my head and back up into the sky. I was scared silly and had to take a break right then and there. A few days later it was revealed that the Martians were Frank and Uncle Everett. They had known that I was out on the tractor. I can only imagine those laughing aliens when they zeroed in on me.

Riding my thumb

I could feel change coming. It felt like diving in deep water on a hot July afternoon. The plunge through the surface was warm, but immediately your whole body tightened from the cool water in the layers below. The heat was washed away as you broke the surface, taking in fresh air. That's what the summer before eighth grade felt like, a new refreshing era energizing my fourteen-year-old spirit. This bracing was fueled by new music like "Rock Around the Clock," "Hound Dog," and "Don't Be Cruel." It all seemed to come together on maple wooden wheels.

Ed and I would spend hours at East Side Park in Washington at the Roller Skating Rink. The rink had a portable laid wooded floor, with a huge canvas tent as a canopy. There was a railing around the perimeter that allowed skaters to mingle with those standing outside. Skaters could rent skates if they didn't have their own. More fashionable skaters brought their own encased in fancy metal skate cases. When opened you would find a set of black leather Hyde roller skates along with wrenches, keys, and oil for the wheels. For girls, the skates might be all white with little embossed roses on the sides. After sunset a mellow yellow light cast a warm glow over the skating lovers, who either held hands or were in each other's arms, skating to the music emanating from the megaphone speakers at each side.

Then there were whirling and twirling maniacs, in their black and white "Zipees," performing fancy tricks and skating backward and forward. That would be Ed and me. We were terrors on the wood. From eleven years on, Ed and I were standard participants at this rink. And not to brag but we were good. It was about that time when I began to notice the girls in their tight shorts and skating skirts. It became obvious to me that I needed to work more so I could buy a pair of white buck shoes. They were called "bucks" since they were made from buckskin, but typically they were suede. (A man named Carl Perkins would croon about the blue ones.) White bucks were hard to keep cleaned but that teen heartthrob, Pat Boone, made it clear to me that skating like a fanatic wasn't going to get me up close and personal to those long-legged, pony-tailed skating gals as much as white bucks.

So at fourteen I signed up for a social security number. Ed signed up with me (we were just one number apart). We needed the cards for a well-paid seasonal summer job. It was watermelon-picking time, and the job I wanted was over in Knox County, in the sandy hills of Decker Township, where the west fork of the White River ties into the Wabash River.

The job was piecemeal. We loaded wagons and trucks that crawled along the rows of melons. My home was there at the melon farms in a row of shanties built of tin roofs and rough cut native lumber tacked on the sides. There wasn't much more room than there would be in a coffin to lie down and sleep. The only good thing about these migrant bungalows was that Ed and I shared one together and didn't have to sleep with the gypsies. Several of the gypsy families worked together picking the melons. There was no slacking. Each truck had a crew boss, and he let you know that you were expected to be heaving those green-striped melons as quickly as everyone else. We had the option to work by the hour, but we would be paid way less. Being paid by the truckload was better. There were bonuses for extra loaded trucks so we had an incentive to work together—and harder. I learned a great lesson on labor management by working those fields and watching different styles of motivation.

There were plenty of busted melons. We could reach in and grab the heart, eating as we crossed the fields. After a while, though, the melon hearts didn't hold their previous thrill. Ed and I passed melon seeds for a month after we finished that job. The melon migration moved north, and the Harrawood migrants hitched a ride back to the Basement House.

I was an old pro who had been hitching rides with my thumb since I was fourteen years old, hitchhiking to the drive-in theatre, roller skating rink, and basketball games. Often I would be hiking late into the night to get back home. A stranger or an occasional drunk would stop and offer a ride. I learned to make a quick read of people. I never feared people, because I was too tough—or maybe, too ignorant. Snap calls to accept a ride or not sometimes depended upon weather conditions, or the lateness of the hour. Most of the time I got a ride from people I knew, or who knew my family. So there were only a few instances during those Indiana days that I ever encountered an uneasy ride.

Chapter 6 - The Basment House

One night hitchhiking back from Washington, a ten-wheeler tank truck stopped at an intersection, and the driver offered me a ride. The trucker was a nice enough fellow, but after I told him where I wanted to get off, he said he wasn't going to stop so I'd have to jump from the truck. "Do what?" I asked apprehensively.

"Yeah, I'm not going to stop," he answered. "I'll slow down a bit, but I'm not stopping on the highway." He said this with no mischief in his voice. The trucker explained that he didn't want to stop because of traffic. Okay, it was dark, but you could still see a far piece in both directions, and there weren't any headlights either way.

"Up here is where I'm getting off," I said, pointing up the highway.

"Well get out and stand on the step, and I'll slow down enough for you."

I opened the door, stepped out on the running board, and closed the door. As the truck took off, wind blasted my face, and I felt the occasional whack of a night bug hitting me in the head. I held tight to the braces of his "California mirrors" and prepared to make a running jump. It became painfully apparent that the trucker wasn't going to do any slowing for me. He didn't even hit his brakes. Okay, either Tom hangs on the side of this tanker for the next however many miles or …JUMP!

When I landed I was clearing out the ditch through a series of rolls and summersaults, with the flash of an angry monkey in an alley years ago racing across my mind. I picked myself up, spit out grass and gravel from my mouth, and watched the amber taillights of that truck disappear into the darkness. I am certain I heard a deep belly laugh coming out of the exhaust stacks.

There were many nights when I caught rides and got off at that same point in blind-pitch darkness. The only way to keep from walking off into the side ditch, while heading back to the Basement House, was by feeling the gravel under my feet. Traffic on the road pushed the gravel to the center and along the edge. By keeping the gravel to one side or another while walking, I was able to stay on the road. If I wandered from the gravel I knew I was off course and adjusted by finding the gravel line again—night navigation.

One night, Ed and I were just in sight of highway U.S. 50 as we headed north up the dusty gravel road. We were hitching a ride to the roller rink. We heard a vehicle come up behind us. It was Frank. "You boys forget to do something?" he asked.

"Well, don't think so." We instinctively knew that this was going to be another one of Frank's lessons of life.

"Get in." So we scooted inside of his truck, and he took us back to the Basement House, where Frank had rigged up a shower, of sorts. He walked us in and said, "Is that where you leave the wash rag?" The wash rag was down on the shower floor, so I picked it up and hung it up nicely. Frank didn't make one comment.

Crisis averted, we walked the familiar mile up to the highway. We were about the same distance as before when we heard that familiar engine sound.

"Did you forget something?"

"No!" Both Ed and I answered in chorus.

"Get in." So we scooted back in for the second time. We pulled in the drive, and he took us back to the shower. "Is this where the soap goes?" The soggy Ivory bar was right there on the floor. I picked it up, placed it where it belonged, and systematically performed a serious check over the bathroom and our bedroom. Again, Ed and I headed back up to the highway but at a faster pace. And as soon as we got halfway there, we jumped off the road and cut through the woods. It was a little longer and rougher with briars, weeds, ticks and chiggers, but this evasion plan got us clear of

Chapter 6 - The Basment House

our adversary.

I first learned the taste of whiskey from Frank's stash. Somehow, he won a full gallon of whiskey, with a very handy pump dispenser right on top. When coon-hunting season arrived, my brothers and I would pump out enough to liven up the night hunts. We were ever so clever. By just replacing what we took with water, who could tell the difference? One night a little whiskey, another night a little whiskey, and another night a little whiskey. After a while, though, even we could determine the whiskey was being watered down, and who could ever fool a connoisseur like Frank?

We got caught. Unimaginably, our rear ends weren't handed to us. Yes sir, we did receive a stern fatherly lecture; not for taking the whiskey, but for watering it down! "Don't be water'n' down good whiskey," Frank spoke to us in a manner that would hopefully appeal to us philosophically. There are some things men just don't desecrate.

Mom was one who never let dreams die; for her it was implicit that "there was no business like show business." Her brush with stardom in Chicago only steeled her desire to develop the raw talent she knew her kids held inside. She just always believed that one of us would dazzle the world with a Broadway performance.

There were no tortures imaginable that would have gotten Ed or me to do what she was able to have our "little" brother Jimmie and Lois do, which was to take tap dancing lessons.

From the very beginning it was painful to witness these sessions in the Basement House. They could not end soon enough as far as I was concerned. With Mom's new portable automatic record player and that monotone beat played over and over, it put us all in a maddened state.

Jim and Lois were at arm's length, side by side. "Okay let's begin. A one…a two…and a three…Shuffle… Slide… and Kick … one-two-three,

Shuffle… Slide… Kick, one-two-three." Even Pepper the dog moaned when Jim made his not-so-dainty kick. Anyone who painfully observed these sessions knew that no amount of "shuffle, slide, or kick" would ever make Jimmie a future Fred Astaire. It was unspeakable. Frank walked in on one of these sessions, stared for a few moments, turned around, and headed right back to town.

An inside family joke was that Jim couldn't afford tap dancing shoes so he put rocks between his toes to make the tapping sound. At a recital Jim did one of his kicks, and a rock flew from his toes and knocked out a lady in the audience. That's the story, anyway!

During this time, Gayle was working for Mr. Norman, collecting milk from the Amish farms. Gayle enlisted me as his grunt man, preparing me to take his place. This required lots of simple hard work and getting up long before the roosters. I lifted, carried, and loaded ten-gallon metal cans that weighed twenty-five pounds empty. When full they were right at one hundred pounds. These cans were two feet tall and a foot wide, with an opening of eight inches at the top, which was sealed by a metal stopper. They had five-inch grips on each side. I had a trick to hoisting these cans up into the truck. I'd grab the handles and swing the can, like throwing a discus. But, if I also lifted with my knee I could leverage the can upward more easily. Sometimes a loose stopper flew off and drench me in milk.

The milking was all done by hand, and it was near the cusp of seeing the last days of these small dairy farms. Government was moving in with regulations that would eventually suffocate these family enterprises. Some families had two cans of milk to sell each day, while others had up to four. In each case, though, it was entirely a family effort with the girls often doing the milking. These dairymaids would grab their three-legged milking stools and swing them in behind, while simultaneously bunching their long plain pastel dresses up between their legs and tucking their heads into the side of the cow. The maid's firm grip squeezed the cow's teats, and a "sprit sprit" sound of the milk hitting the buckets carried through the barn. When the bucket was full they would strain the milk into the cans.

The Amish had no electricity but it was essential that the milk be cooled so they used windmills to pump cool water to small block houses near the windmills. The water flowed through a concrete trough deep enough for the water to rise just below the stopper lid. The water then circulated back into the well to be cooled again. This system kept the milk as cool as any milk in an electric refrigerator, and the Amish kept their perishable food stuff stored there, too.

The roads in the Amish "settlement" were literally horse and buggy roads with little to no gravel. Deep ruts that cut into the mocha-colored clay of Barr Township made driving a truck difficult even in fair weather and almost impossible in wet weather. When the roads were dry, man and beast choked on the dust. There were many times that the Amish pulled our truck through mud with a team of their draft horses.

Milk was hauled in a single axle "dually" with a boxed bed. Our load was about fifty cans, more or less. The milk was hauled west forty miles to Vincennes, Indiana, on the Wabash River. There, a tester would knock off the lids with a mallet and, with a long-handled test spoon, randomly test the milk. He would sip from the spoon, swish it around in his mouth, spit it out, and check another. Once this was done I unloaded to another dairyman who set them on a conveyer belt as they traveled down to where other men dumped the milk into a vat. The cans were turned upside down and steam washed. Next, we would take the truck around back to reload our cans. Three bucks for the job and I was glad to get it.

Back Words

Photographs

W.A. Harrawood, Elise Valentine Harrawood, Frank Harrawood - February 1916.

Clockwise from upper left: Everett Harrawood, Leo Harrawood, Frank Harrawood, Paul Harrawood. Center: W.A. and Elise Harrawood.

Back Words

Top row: Grandma Elise Harrawood, Paul Harrawood, Everett Harrawood, W.A. Harrawood. Bottom row: Laura Rose Harrawood, Frank Harrawood, Nellie Harrawood. Gladys is looking over Grandma's shoulder.

Center row (l-r): Tom Harrawood, Frank Harrawood (holding Jimmy), Mom (holding Lois), Ed Harrawood. Gayle Harrawoood is standing in the back row.

Aunt Auggie Harrawood with Gary Harrawood sitting on Old John, the mule, 1950.

Mom and Frank with Tom stainding on the boom of the dragline.

Mom and Frank in front of his Charter Bus.

Tom and Jimmy Harrawood with Ed Scott, 1956.

Back Words

East 50 Drive-In Theater, 1950.

Center - Company Commander Nixon. Tom Harrawood is standing at Nixon's right arm, July 26, 1960.

Back Words

RCPO Tom Harrawood leading his company and calling cadence for, "Passing in Review," 1960.

Tom's ship, LST 1166 in South Korea awaiting troops.

Tom in Seattle, Washington.

Wood Waste Energy owners (l-r): Greg Smith, Tom Harrawood, Alan Stone.

Jim Spiegal, Tom Harrawood, Greg Smith, Alan Stone.

Tom and Sandy.

Back Words

CHAPTER SEVEN

The Last Days of Hoosier School

I always kept hard-earned money in my pockets throughout the eighth grade. I never turned down an opportunity to make a dollar, and I was in full "tom- foolery" mode with my partners. I used some of that money during my last semester at the 1957 Basketball Sectional, which was played in Washington. An episode during that sectional sent the whole Montgomery school community into an uproar. For me, it offered a lucrative learning experience.

Friday afternoon, on the first day of March, our team was playing the Washington Hatchets. I was there in the cheering block, more intent on flirting with the girls in the stands than watching the game itself. Washington Fire Chief Daily and a policeman walked over to the Montgomery school superintendent. The seriousness of the conversation was not immediately apparent. However, when the super turned and quickly engaged some of the other community members, a trickle of folks began to file out of the bleachers. The word spread across our Viking section, moving people like wind blowing across a wheat field. "THE SCHOOL IS ON FIRE!" The bleachers emptied.

Washington Daily Times, Saturday March 2, 1957, Headline:
BARR TWP. SCHOOL DESTROYED BY FIRE
$200,000 Loss

Austin Grannan, the school custodian, was washing windows at two o'clock Friday afternoon when he discovered the fire. Austin noticed plumes of black smoke drifting down the halls from the direction of the boiler room. A gallant effort was made by Austin trying to control the fire, going through two fire extinguishers. The flames clawed wildly upward and burst through the roof. A March wind picked up and acted like a bellows, increasing the intensity. The fire was out of control.

Chief Daily and his Washington firefighters were first on the scene, followed by Loogootee and then Montgomery volunteers. A local writer in the Washington Daily wrote, "Bright red fire consumed the 32-year-old building, while the eight-cylinder engine of a 1923 Birsch fire-truck chugged its heart out to save it."

The four-inch water lines at the school could not produce adequate pressure or enough water needed. Eventually, five hundred gallons per minute was being pumped from Montgomery's recently new water tank. It was just not enough to save the school. Northeast of the school (about twelve hundred yards) was a pond, and water was pumped from it. Because of this, the gymnasium on the north side of the school was saved.

Saturday, crowds gathered to gaze upon the smoldering ruins, while school kids rejoiced and shot hoops on the outside ball court. Concerned citizens wondered "what are the students to do with only eight weeks of school remaining?" Others were already assigning blame: The boiler room was unsafe! There were lots of defects! I've heard that the superintendent wanted it to burn! Still others were discussing the sectional game and how it was that Montgomery lost to Washington, 54 to 39. But my brother Ed played brilliantly, scoring fifteen points before fouling out of the game.

One hundred eighty upper classmen and one hundred fifty grade school students had, according to the state superintendent of schools, just ten days of classes remaining. We were out for a week, but for the remaining school year it was decided that the lower grade school classes would be split between Washington schools. The seventh and eighth grades would drive to Cannelburg while upper classes would attend classes at the Washington National Guard Armory.

During my last days of eighth grade, I sat right back in Cannelburg where it all started. Our teacher accompanied us and began preparing for final exams. A new type of test would provide a comparison with other schools in the state. The day of the test, an administrator and my teacher singled out Popper, Freak, Simon, and me and took us aside. It was explained that we would never do anything other than operate bulldozers or be farm laborers. Furthermore, we would only lower the overall test scores "so go out and play ball," they said. With no hesitation, we followed their suggestion. This is how I ended nine years of grade school.

Immediately after school was let out, Ed and I seized the opportunity to make money by scrapping the remains of the burnt out school. Off and on we had been gathering scrap metal and doing salvage work on old mining structures and dilapidated buildings. The two of us ran the numbers on the effort and put together a proposal for a bid. A good return on our investment was possible. The only problem was that we didn't have the money to make a bid. The two of us approached Frank and made our pitch, but Frank was not a gambler on such ventures. Ed and I came at him from every angle, and finally he consented. Whether he pulled the money from his sock drawer or got it from our local banker, we don't know but he came up with five hundred dollars. A bid of five hundred dollars for the salvage rights was offered, and we won.

Ed and I jumped right on it, removing the metal desk, wiring, and every high-dollar material we could find, but then we were stopped. The authorities said that we were not allowed to work the project since we were under 18 years old. So it was back to an Ed and Tom conference. Our solution was to cut in a man who dealt in scrap material from down south about twenty miles. He operated out of Jasper, Indiana. We were ready to "knee cap" Frank who just didn't want anything to do with it, so Ed and I went down ourselves and pitched the proposal. The deal was made. He provided a crane, trucks, and a laborer. Ed and I worked on smaller pieces out in the courtyard. In the end the job was completed to requirements, and we made fifteen hundred dollars. A check was cut and sent to Frank. We never got to divide up our share—the thousand bucks—between Ed and me. Frank took back the five hundred we owed him and kept the rest. He gave us a minuscule slice of the pie. Maybe Frank used it to benefit the family, or maybe not. He got himself a nice new suit out of it, and he boasted at the bars of his savvy business acumen. Ed and I came to appreciate each other's talents, and our abilities to develop and implement successful business deals. We never forgot that.

Like a stray dog I was shooed on down the road to freshman year in the Armory. Our class motto was "we're in the Armory now." The Armory provided a kitchen that became the home economics class. It had six other rooms for classes and one more for an office. Essentially, the bulk of the Armory was a gymnasium that was used by guardsmen for the weekend drills. In the center a makeshift study hall was created, and along the edges they fashioned more classrooms. Books and desks were provided by the surrounding schools.

My first year in high school was fairly normal with one exception: That October there was a certain amount of "Red Scare" going around about the Soviet "Sputnik" satellite. But hey, I was a freshman now, so how did that really concern me? Like all the freshmen classes before us, we held a class meeting and elected officers. The first order of business was how to raise money for our class trips. The days of students making sales pitches for subscriptions to monthly magazines—forcing grandparents, uncles, aunts, friends, and neighbors to buy or donate through guilt, or standing at street intersections with buckets and begging—hadn't started. We actually went out and worked for our funds. One of those ways was gleaning corn fields. The old-style corn pickers, while much better than hand shucking, still knocked down or missed many of the corn stalks. This gave us an opportunity to glean lots of fields. Community farmers were rather generous with the classes.

To glean a field was exactly what it sounded like. We would each take a row and walk it to the end, looking for missed ears and stepping on husks to make sure there were no ears inside. Everyone carried a burlap bag, and each of us boys maneuvered to be along the row of the cutest girls. It was a wholesome, fun-filled day, and we made money doing it.

The curriculum at school was divided into three categories: "Academic" was designed for college bound students; "Commercial" was designed for students going to work in business and saleable ventures; and "Agriculture," which was for me.

I, as a matter of fact, had done very well with this. The courses consisted of welding, machinery, mechanical application, livestock management, grain production, and business math. These things called more for manipulation of tools and a common-sense approach toward problems. I was not to be outdone when it came to "wrenching and welding." Mix an assortment of seeds and I'd be quick to sort out alfalfa, buckwheat, clover (red or white), corn, soybeans, timothy, and lespedeza. But you'd find me in the outhouse when it came to writing any of this down on a test. I could instruct you when to plant, how to plant, and what to plant. I could tell you the correct spacing, proper amount of fertilizer, and how much hay was in a round stack, but I couldn't write it down on paper.

Perhaps because of the novelty of going to school at the Armory, and probably because of the internecine battles being fought over the new school, my first high school year went by in a blur.

Montgomery School was being targeted for consolidation because of its age, its oiled floors, and the great cost to bring it up to state specifications. It would have been a tenuous fight for the school community against the state's argument for consolidation. On the other hand, it would have been even more of a problem to convince the taxpayers, especially those who paid property taxes, to build a new school. The school fire put a whole different argument on the table. Heated debates during school board meetings over the future of Montgomery School could quickly approach fist fights. Neighbors verbally fought with each other over how the school should be built, or if it should be built at all. In the end the fight went in the direction of a new school, including a new gymnasium, even though the old school gym was saved from the fire. And so the fire actually saved the school. Eight years later, Alfordsville School closed and consolidated with a modern Montgomery School to make the new Barr-Reeve Township School.

"He's in the jailhouse now"

In 1958 I turned sixteen and took the exam to obtain a driver's license. If my educators would have given me a test like the driver's test, they would have felt a bit more justified in scooting me up to the next grade. At my request the test was read to me, a service provided by law. I passed with a score over seventy percent.

I had a new lease on life, just as anyone who had turned sixteen and earned the privilege to drive would. The possibilities seemed endless in my calculations. I had all kinds of plans. Just a few weeks after being "certified," I got the '55 Plymouth for the night. Jim and I were out and about just cruising, when we ran into an old friend of ours who was on leave from the Marines. Kenny was a lanky sort of guy, but as tough as an old hickory. Jim and I were glad to have him on board, especially when he produced a bottle of whiskey. The three of us were out on the back roads, sipping whiskey and laughing at all the bull that Kenny was laying on us. Then, back in town we went to get another bottle, and we were out on the back roads again. Things started getting a little blurry from here on. I remember climbing a windmill and seeing a lot of people down below telling me to get back down. I remember someone passing me a fifth of whiskey, and I remember tipping it up and sucking down the whiskey like it was mother's milk. I had become incapacitated enough that somewhere Kenny took over the driving part. The next thing I remember, I was laying in the back seat and semiconsciously experiencing something of a toss and roll, and then the whirling of spinning tires.

I vaguely remember looking up and seeing a church steeple. For whatever reason, Kenny had to drive to Loogootee, and for another mystifying reason, Kenny had to drive over a concrete embankment along the steps of the entrance to St. John's Catholic Church. We were in luck, though, after Jim and Kenny hid the booze in a nearby shrub. Some of the parishioners who were attending a forty-eight-hour service came out as we called for help to push the car off of the wall. I sobered up just enough that I could lay across the floor board while pushing on the brake with my hand. This I also remembered: Kenny talking me into admitting I was the driver because it would be detrimental to his Marine career. Well "Semper Fi"! Anything for a serviceman.

The next thing I knew I was handcuffed and staggering toward the police car. When we got to the city lockup, the town marshal made me stand in front of a door, and he stood behind me. There was a yellow light above the door as he pushed a buzzer, and when it seemed that no one was going to answer, I spun around and remarked that "no one's home so let's go." That's when I was twirled around and slammed into the wall, getting a good taste of the green paint. The marshal told me in so many words to shut up.

Jim, because of his age, was held upstairs in the women's cell. Kenny was in the opposite cell from me. Between our cells was something of a bullpen separating us.

It was my first brush with the law and the first time I found myself in a jail house with a tremendous hangover. I was greeted the next morning with black coffee and matching toast, with a runny egg looking up at me. I could not bear the sight of this jailhouse breakfast, much less be able to eat it. But Kenny ravished both his and mine. The jailers put a lunatic inside the bullpen who walked back and forth, repeating over and over AND over, "What, what, what."

My pounding head could hardly take it, and it must have irritated Kenny as well. Kenny shouted out to the man, "What…what…what! What the hell are you a light bulb?"

Sometime in the afternoon Frank came and bailed us out. I was certain of a forthcoming execution, but to my surprise, other than a "what an idiot you are" type lecture, it was rather calm.

Not so with the law; they took my license, and I assumed it would be forever. In thirty days I was in front of the marshal and admitted that I wasn't driving. He said that he had known that and did not turn my license into the state. The marshal asked, "How much money do you have?" I told him I had saved up one hundred twelve dollars to buy a motorcycle. The marshal unsympathetically announced that my fine just happened to be one hundred twelve dollars. I got my driving privileges back and never again slept overnight in a jail cell. The marshal, who was our family insurance agent, taught me the best lesson of this incident.

"This too shall pass," the good book said, and in no time I was driving that good old '55 to the movies, often with my buddies, whistling the theme to Bridge on the River Kwai, or with an arm around my date as "Love Letters in the Sand" flowed from the radio and set the mood. I looked down at my scuffed up white buck shoes and wondered how better—really—could life get? going into my sophomore year.

Supplementing my agricultural courses in my second year of high school was the organization that every boy in the ag field joined: the Future Farmers of America (FFA). I vigorously participated in the FFA, and I enjoyed all the meetings and functions. I was quite proud to wear the blue corduroy jacket with the cross section of an ear of corn on the back emblazoned with "FFA Montgomery Indiana Chapter." I scored high in FFA contests and made money for the club by varmint hunting and gathering feral cats.

The universities were paying three dollars for every feral cat that we furnished, so Jim and I, along with some friends, got to use Mom's '55 Plymouth to round up cats. We'd chase them down, stuff them in a gunny sack, carry them to the car, and put them in the trunk. Finding stray cats was not as big a task as one might think; they were usually at every farmhouse. That's why we would stop and ask if they had any that they wanted to get rid of. We stopped at one farmhouse and asked if there were any to be had. This gruff old farmer said "no, I don't have any cats."

As we were walking out of the driveway, Jim saw a cat sitting on a post. He grabbed it and threw it in the trunk as he exclaimed, "Well he says he don't have any."

We even snatched up an opossum and tossed it in the trunk. It was a good haul. The catnappers needed refreshments and needed to refuel the Plymouth. We pulled into a gas station at Loogootee. For some reason Jim thought he needed to open the trunk, and when he did cats sprang out of the trunk like jack-in-the-box toys. A tractor with a trailer happened by at that moment and took one of our specimens. The squished cat wasn't the only casualty, because a few days later we got to smelling something under the rear seat. After a serious exploration, we found that 'possum still very much alive under the rear seat.

Westward Bound

If Americans were concerned about Ike's recent heart attack, they didn't voice it during the 1956 election. But there was a good bit of concern over the economic recession blanketing America during these days. The old General, during his second political campaign, was reminiscing about his 1919 adventure. Ike, along with an Army caravan, embarked from the White House to cross America to San Francisco, California. It took two months at an average of five miles an hour to travel the 3,350 miles. Ike elaborated on the need to develop the highways in America. President Eisenhower said that he would have the democrat-held House send him a bill to increase road building funds, and, being politicians, they recognized electioneering candy. The bill passed. Ike didn't father the interstate system, but he sure got it moving; and because of it, he was re-elected. This started an economic boom that would change the American landscape along with the culture for years to come.

Frank and his employer, Bridges Paving Company, out of St. Louis, Missouri, benefited from that road stimulus. At first he began working for them seasonally, just on the other side of the Wabash River, in Illinois. Soon more bids were let, and the company began moving back toward the west. Frank had been living in hotels and sleeping rooms and would come home on weekends. But by 1959 he would be full time, and Frank was going with the company.

I may have been the flotsam of the local educational system, maybe a bit callow, a smidgen of a wiseacre, and to my teachers, just an outright horror, but when I walked out of those new double doors of Montgomery School in the spring of 1959, I was absolutely sure of one thing: A man must earn his way, and—by God—Thomas Earl Harrawood was a man!

And so that very spring, on my seventeenth birthday, Frank came up to me and asked, "Tom, we need a man to work a jackhammer over in Olney. You want the work?" He asked me as if I had an alternative.

Olney, Illinois, was every bit of a hundred miles from our Basement House. Olney—home of the white squirrel—was smack dab in the middle of the most concentrated area of these famed squirrels. Frank and some of the crew had acquired some sleeping rooms from a little old lady with a talking parrot. The landlady's parrot was taught to swear from the truckers, earning them a quick eviction. I would bunk with Frank, an experience that would prepare one to sleep in any condition. His hot, sour whiskey breath scratched at my neck, and his flopping arms smacked me in the head. And that escaping gas, reeking of pickled boiled eggs with just a pinch of pickled pigs' feet from off the bar counter, I must admit, produced some staggering dreams.

I worked with a group of tireless men, and one, in particular, intrigued me. He was our paving operator and an American Indian. This man had survived the Bataan Death March, and had a back full of unholy scars inflicted by Japanese bayonets and clubs.

Tucking a jackhammer into your stomach and punching at concrete all day on Illinois highway 130, with acrid concrete dust plugging up your nose, was work—hard work. I realized that this was the station in life of a man who could not read or write. It was just like remembering what being left behind in the second grade felt like. Again, the heavy hand of reality slapped me on the side of the head.

Accompanying Frank in bars after working hours, and being embarrassed by his shenanigans, was all worthwhile on the day that my paycheck arrived. One hundred and fifty dollars! For a man who worked just as hard, and made only three dollars a day! I held on to that check for as long as I could because it felt so good.

In due course the job ended, and Frank was offered a full-time position as master mechanic. Eventually, he would become superintendent. The company returned to St. Louis, and Frank was going with them, and he had made the decision to take us all along.

CHAPTER EIGHT

Departure

A shotgun wasn't observed, but one most likely lay nearby when Gayle Harrawood went to the church (willingly) with Darlene McAtee, a Montgomery girl, to exchange marriage vows. After the wedding, the newlyweds bought a stubby little trailer that they parked beside the Basement House. Gayle worked at various pursuits until he was hired via Frank to work for Bridges Paving. Then Gayle and Darlene moved and resettled across the Mississippi River in the St. Ann area where Gayle worked at Bridges asphalt plant. The Harrawoods established their first "beach head" in Missouri.

Ed, on the other hand, quit school before his senior year and joined the Navy. Serving in San Diego, Ed was notified that his girlfriend's parents did have a shotgun. Ed requested leave to get married, and he came back home in his Navy Blues. His bride was Doris Bullock, and with an agreement between the two, they set a date. However, Ed was not allowed to wear his Dress Blues for the ceremony, nor was he allowed entrance through the front doors of the Catholic church. So Ed unceremoniously came in from a side door, and they exchanged vows. He returned to the California base and began arrangements for Doris Harrawood to follow.

That left Jim, Lois, and me carrying our belongings up out of the Basement House. Mom stuffed everything she needed, including Pepper the dog, in every cubbyhole she could find. This struck me as reminiscent of our California trip seven years earlier. Frank packed his 1957 blue

Chevrolet Apache work truck and hitched a trailer to it. Since Frank was the last one to walk up out of the Basement House, he then locked the door.

The blue truck and its trailer headed up to U.S. Route 50. Behind that, the red and white 1955 Plymouth followed, as both left behind a low churning trail of gravel dust drifting over the Basement. There was a toot of the horn as we passed the Scott farm. The caravan stopped at the highway, turned left, and began a journey of close to 200 miles to Missouri. I had slept my last night in the Basement House.

As we traversed through Montgomery, I was stretching my neck to catch a glimpse of any of my cornfield rebels but saw none. There was no violent storm, but an economic tempest had just uprooted my life. In spite of anticipating this new adventure, I was leaving behind my history and I wondered what the future held for me. Would I be accepted in school? Would I even go to school? After all I was seventeen! I did not know what was being said in the truck, but in the car I was in, there was quiet introspection; at least I do not remember much talk. I mulled over many possible scenarios coming my way, as we crossed over the Wabash River on the George Rogers Clark Bridge. I glanced outside and saw the last reflection of Indiana from the side mirror.

Bridgeton

The Missouri River crawls out from Kansas City and winds itself eastward across central Missouri. Then it flows south to the capital, Jefferson City. There it continues northeastward forming a hump at Herman, where it moves to the south toward Washington. Here it makes a long graceful arch to the northeast wrapping itself up and over the top of the greater St. Louis area like the head of a rising cobra striking at the Mis-

Chapter 8 - Departure

sissippi River. Imagine this confluence at the twelve o'clock position with the center of the clock being St. Louis. The Mississippi River then flows straight south to Jefferson Barracks, at six o'clock. From twelve to six, and to the West, is the greater St. Louis area. Bridgeton is at ten o'clock and the Missouri River there is the rising snake's back. On Bridgeton's side of the "Mighty Mo" is St. Louis County, while across the river is St. Charles and St. Charles County.

From the center of the clock the hour hand is pointed straight at ten. On that line is the St. Louis Lambert International Airport runway in Bridgeton. At the very end of that runway is where Frank moved us. When we arrived in mid-summer of 1959, its greatest growth had just kicked off. New single family homes were being built by the thousands; however, none of these new homes would be ours. No, Frank did not disappoint us in his selection of our new abode; it was literally right at the end of the runway. Late at night the caravan pulled into the drive of our Bridgeton home. (I think Frank planned it that way). There was haste in moving inside. Mattresses were flopped down on the floor.

Air traffic was minimal with only an occasional craft gliding out of the Missouri night sky and over our rooftop with a noticeable shutting down of the engine. It seemed bearable. I was in deep sleep when the runway pattern was reversed and the first twin engine turboprop came roaring up off the runway. I swear it had to be peeling off the roof shingles. I rolled off of my mattress and tried to find my way to the door as I ran into Jim who was fumbling into unfamiliar walls. Pepper was yelping from being stepped on by fleeing occupants. All of us—Lois, Mom, Frank, Jim and I—ran out of the house, for there was nothing but certainty that we were being bombed by the Russians. There was a little swearing and some laughter as the refugees clambered back inside.

The next day we were assigned our sleeping quarters. Mom, Frank,

Lois, and Pepper were topside; Jim and I were in the basement. My room was a former coal room with its coal chute above my head. I would never have a bed frame here, just a mattress on the floor. It would have been nicer if it afforded more light, but it had fresh paint and, as I found out that second night, it muffled the rooftop takeoffs and approaches of the turboprops. It was suitable enough.

Quick morning looks around the area revealed that the houses were all built alike—small cottages constructed in the late thirties to early forties. The area residents that I met were all rather friendly, but when you said anything to them they always replied by saying "Huh?" This local area was gray from age, and it took no genius to realize that no new houses were planned to be built in this area. There was only one direction that the airport could eventually expand.

The airplanes coming and going absolutely captivated Jim and me. Being free-range Hoosiers who ventured into any woods or field, the two of us headed right over to the runway and lay on the edge where the planes took off or touched down. A Piper Cub was the biggest aircraft we had ever been around, so being just feet from these massive planes was exhilarating for us. We did this for about a week before security chased us off.

Behind the Bridges asphalt plant was a shingle company. Gayle was familiar with the shingle plant manager and arranged a job for me. I offloaded from the railcars, but soon was moved to the labeling department. However, they found out I couldn't read so they sent me over to bust open bags of lime and dump them on a conveyer that went up to a bin. When the lime started spilling down on my head, I knew that it was full. They assigned me a fire billet, but during a drill I started spraying with a high-pressure fire hose, knocking windows out of the plant, so back to the bins I went. The pay was good but the work was mighty dirty and hot. The shingle job only lasted for a few weeks, but I stayed with the job right up until school started. At that point I had prospects for another job as a carhop at Steak and Shake.

Pattonville High

My charming Indiana personality quickly enabled me to acquire a clique of friends who clued me in on the local scene. I was introduced to the carhop gig. Though a bit hesitant at first, I was advised that carhopping was a profitable occupation. So I applied at Steak and Shake just over on St. Charles Rock Road.

Steak and Shake originally came out of Normal Illinois in the mid-1930s. It was started by Gus Belt who promoted his business plainly enough by marketing freshly ground steakburgers. Gus would wait until his business was full and then push a cart full of T-bones and sirloin steaks past the customers and in full sight grind them up making the famous steakburgers. Gus then added curb service, and soon after this he sold his first franchise.

It was my first full uniform. I proudly wore white pants, a black cummerbund belt with an attached letter holder, a white shirt, and a black bowtie topped with a white Steak and Shake hat trimmed in black. The order tickets were preprinted, and after studying them over it was easy enough to take an order. I carried change in the belt and in my pockets.

My first night went well, even though I was being nudged out by experienced hops that recognized good tippers. Yet I had a lucrative first night; I made nearly six dollars on tips alone. I could raise a family on this kind of money. An incident a few days later gave me faith and trust in humanity. A car pulled into one of my territorial slots and I took their order. It came to a little less than three dollars, but they didn't have the money. I told them that it was okay, just come back sometime this week and pay me. My country "upbringing" led me to believe them when they said they would come back with the money. The other hops gave me a good hissing, "You'll never see them again. What a rube you are." But wouldn't you know it; they did come back that evening with the money and gave me a fifty cent tip to boot. Nevertheless, that was the last time I provided such free generosity. I pocketed their tip as I walked past the other hops and flashed a big Thomas Earl grin.

It didn't take long before I understood the tip routine, and I became well known as someone who would usually earn a good gratuity. Because of my size and tenacity, I'd cut off any other hop headed toward what I knew as a good customer, quickly snapping down my card on their windshield. Okay Tom, you got that one, too.

I had an unusual foursome that came in every Sunday night, a man and a woman up front and two chimpanzees in the back seat. They always parked in the same slot, which I owned, and the other hops would back off.

"Four hamburgers and two sodas please," would be their standard order.

"Here you go, four hamburgers and two sodas." I handed them the order, and the man would unwrap the burgers and hand one at a time back to the chimps. Those chimps were politer than most children I waited on. I always got a very good tip from the chimpanzee family.

The School of Car Hop's was a good learning experience, with interaction among various personalities. I quickly determined who needed a good joke or a nice compliment, and in return I received a nice tip. Tips came in other forms, too. I had a fellow who tipped me one night with "calling cards" for a house-of-ill-repute in downtown St. Louis. I quickly turned a profit by selling them to other hops or my "preferred customers." I stayed at the carhopping job for the rest of my time at school.

Chapter 8 - Departure

Pattonville School hallways revealed amazing opportunities that I knew I could never attain. Walking down the halls I peered through open doors and saw classrooms with drafting tables and artist easels, model rockets, globes, and space charts. There were rooms with beakers, glass jars, and gas burners. There were rooms with jars of pickled insects and snakes. Without question it was nothing like good old Montgomery High School.

One day I was searching for the football coach's office. Montgomery did not support a football program, and I had great passion to play the game. I knocked on the open door and a curt "come on in" followed.

"Yeah, what can I help you with?" The short, burly, thick-necked coach said.

"Well sir, I'd like to play football," I ardently replied.

The coach and I made small talk about where I was from and so forth. Then he said to me, "If you play football as good as you're built, then you come on out to the practice."

Practice was no picnic, but it was apparent to me that none of these guys ever pitched hay bales, tossed milk cans, or wrestled a milk cow from hell. I listened intently to the play calls and froze the practice plays in my mind, because no one knew I could not read the playbook. And by gosh, come hell, high water, or an interception pass, nobody was going to find out either.

It was the first game of the season, and the coach had me playing on both sides of the line—offense and defense. There were times I pleaded with him to take me out of the game because I was so tired. I could not tell you what position I was playing, but the other side's quarterback had the ball. I broke through their defense, picked up the quarterback with the ball between us, and carried him halfway down to our goalpost. Whistles blew and flags flew from every direction, and then the stadium came to a hush. The only thing I heard was the coach giving me football hell and telling me how much of an idiot he thought I was. Well, okay, I learned the rules as I went.

Once football season was over, I thought I'd go try out for basketball, but that was also the point at which grades came out and mine were way below what was needed to be eligible. My Pattonville Pirate athletic days were over. I, however, earned a jacket with a football letter, and oh how proud of that I was.

Pattonville boys and I became a tight little squad of pirates. There were no party or cruisin' nights that the gang did not invite me along. Once I was invited to join them on a tour of Drury College in Springfield, Missouri, a liberal arts and teacher preparatory college. It was founded in 1873 and affiliated with Congregational Christian Churches.

I so admired the campus life and the excitement bursting from my friends, but my spirit was low. I knew that I would never have that experience for myself. If I ever came close to the "poor ol' Tom" self-pity mode it was that day on the campus of Drury College. On the way back the radio jock was spinning out the hot chart numbers like: "He's got the Whole World in His Hands," "Everything's Coming up Roses," and "High Hopes," but the one that immediately struck a chord with me was "Tom Dooley"!

During this time, it really did seem like this old mud ball called earth was being ripped apart. Fidel Castro kicked Batista out of Cuba, the U.S.S.R. shot Gary Powers' U-2 spy plane out of the sky, and Americans were heartbroken that their president was caught in a lie about it. On the road scruffy beatniks were howling mad, but not nearly as mad as the one-hundred-ten-day striking steelworkers and longshoremen. Finally, with not nearly enough points to graduate in my senior year of high school, I quit. It just seemed appropriate at that point to make a break from ev-

Chapter 8 - Departure

eryone and everything. I made a short drive to the United States Navy Recruiting Station in Ferguson, Missouri.

The Chief Petty Officer guided me to a desk and laid down a list of questions and tests. I know this sounds crazy, but I could barely spell T-h-o-m-a-s; that's how illiterate I was. With Mom's help I brought along a cheat sheet with my name, social security number, birth date, and permanent home address. The Chief, after reviewing the test and my information, was up front with me and let me know that I would probably have a great deal of difficulty with naval personnel in San Diego. But I signed the contract and the Chief administered the oath. And for four years I would be in the Navy. It was June 9, 1960.

I boarded and settled in on a TWA prop plane, known as a Connie. I was with other St. Louis navy enlistees as we lifted up off the runway and flew right over the top of our Bridgeton house. The U.S. Navy adventure had just begun.

Back Words

CHAPTER NINE

Seventy-two

My TWA flight from St. Louis made its approach to San Diego, and like the other passengers I stretched toward the window for a hint at what might greet us. The gray ships were the easiest to recognize from the air, and I wondered which one my brother Ed could be on. The cityscape came rushing up, and a screeching noise of the tires preparing for landing, introduced me to a mid-afternoon in California.

A gray Navy bus met us at the terminal, and the St. Louis enlistees were shuffled over to the U.S. Naval Training Center (NTC San Diego). We were told to stand on a painted line on the floor with our arms at our side. A sailor in all white, with a red-braided cord over his left shoulder and the insignia of a Petty Officer First Class, led us through a corridor. Above the entrance was a sign …

> WELCOME ABOARD
> You are now men of the
> UNITED STATES NAVY

This was called the Receiving and Outfitting Unit, better known as "R and O." We were herded to temporary barracks and given a gray wool blanket for the night. I don't believe any of us undressed; we slept in our civilian clothes. It was still light outside when taps sounded. Not long afterward someone from the entrance shouted, "LIGHTS OUT."

'Oh four thirty hours' sure came quickly, I thought when the lights came on and a commanding voice shouted, "FALL OUT." We were shepherded in a sloppy sort of march over to the mess hall where I was very happy with the breakfast and the portions that were offered. After a not so leisurely breakfast, we were back outside, formed up again, and led to another building. At this point all the buildings looked the same on the outside. But once we were inside this building, it was clear this was a barber shop—no, a shearing station. And there was only one style being offered. This cut, if nothing else, made all of us equal. I had come to know some of the guys, but I hardly recognized them with their peeled heads. It was at this point that the sailor who would become our company commander introduced himself.

The process moved rather quickly from here on. While we were being moved from site to site, we were also learning to march. We were instructed to "lead off with your left," and every time the call came back down, we would hear, "Yoour left … yoour right … left … right … Your other right, you idiot." We were learning a marching cadence that was thirty inches in length and one hundred twenty steps to the minute. If the marching orders were for example, "To the right flank, march …" then the order "march" is given on the right foot. A bit confusing at the start, but it was amazing how quickly the company came together. We picked up other things, too, like we didn't talk while in lines or formation.

We were marched over to the clothing check where we were fitted for our boondockers, which are low-cut laced boots. Then we were issued our first set of bell-bottom denim dungarees and a chambray long-sleeved shirt. A set of white boxer shorts and t-shirts, a black-webbed belt with a brass roller buckle, and a blue ball cap completed the issue for now. We were told to change and were given a box so we could send home our civilian clothes. Later, we would be measured for and issued the rest of our seafaring gear. It was at this point that our primary company was marched to our new home— a spacious, sparkling clean barracks. I haven't seen hospitals this clean. I was amazed at how much room we had, though we slept in double bunk beds. There was a wonderful bathroom, what we would call "the head." It had wall-to-wall (or as it was now termed, bulkhead-to-bulkhead) showers, sinks with mirrors, and a line of toilets.

The first two weeks was crammed full of learning. We learned how to make up a bunk the Navy Way, how to fold clothes the Navy Way, how to eat the Navy Way, and even how to poop and brush our teeth the Navy Way. We were instructed on how to walk and talk, and address officers and senior enlisted personnel and females, the Navy Way. We had our chest X-rayed, our teeth x-rayed, and our rear ends checked out. I had inoculations for things I had never heard of. And in the evening, we hand-scrubbed our clothes outside.

Navy life was right darn good for me, so far. I was familiar with being called an idiot, and to me there was nothing unusual about receiving orders or instructions with every insulting name you ever heard tossed at you, along with some new ones. I made the right decision in joining the Navy, and I was sure that I would become a good sailor. But a terrible and confusing turn of events changed my contentment to pure torment. We were marched over to the General Classification Testing (GCT) room.

I had no way of knowing what forms I was filling out, without asking. I was unable to smuggle a cheat sheet in. I sure as hell couldn't copy as we were set in long rows of tables with individual cubbyholes partitioned on all three sides. And if I was able to copy, heck, I might have copied Joe Smith as my name. The GCT test was administered, and all of this was under a time limit. There were sailors in their blue jumpers that roamed, watching and answering any questions. I didn't know what a panic attack was, but here in front of me was my greatest fear—my "Achilles heel" of life. It was a written exam.

The test was divided into parts: English, reading, grammar, and spelling were included in the first part. When multiple choices were given, I made my "best (uneducated) guess." The next part was mathematical, and I worked the problems up to where I had no idea what "find x" meant. The only part offering a reasonable chance of success was the practical section, where I was asked to explain gear process and reductions; leverage and fulcrum applications, and the mechanical aspects; and types of tools and their applications. When the test was over I had nothing left inside but apprehension. There was a break, and at this point we had individual classification interviews. I was asked questions about my previous experiences and what I was hoping to "strike for" in the Navy. My answers were all being typed out by the sailor asking them.

My company and I returned to the barracks, and in a couple of days I was called out and told to report to the GCT offices.

I was shown into a room where a couple of Officers sat behind a desk. I stood at attention before these men. One officer spoke up, "Recruit, do you know that you only scored 72 on the GCT? We're going to put you out of the Navy."

My legs became weak and my stomach was leaden. For a moment I was speechless, a drowning man just tossed a rock. There was nothing left inside but to beg. "No, no, please sir you can't throw me out. Surely there is something I can do in the Navy. I'll do anything asked of me. I'll make a good sailor. Please don't throw me out." There was a quiet conversation between the officers as they dismissed me.

I returned to the barracks and was told to clear out my locker, take my seabag, and report to a new company. During two weeks I had bonded with these guys and now I was leaving. There were no goodbyes, no "see ya around" well-wishes; I was just packed and moved out.

Chapter 9 - Seventy-two

To my surprise, I was assigned to a company of Filipinos! I stood a full foot and a half taller than the tallest of them. For two miserable weeks I marched around with these guys, who were short yet tough recruits. I felt like my shining white-skinned head against their dark skins was a beacon for everyone on the grinder to see and wonder why I was there. My heart would sink when I would see my old company marching by. I would try to become invisible.

I laid there in a barracks full of men I had nothing in common with, and I was sure they deliberately spoke in a foreign tongue when I was around; they wanted nothing to do with me. Of all the many times I listened to taps, there never was a time that taps ever sounded as forlorn or soul-wrenching as these trying evenings. I prayed. "Oh Lord, help me out of this, anything but this, just don't throw me out of the Navy." I tell you there has never been a deeper nor darker time in my life.

Company 257

My prayers were answered. I was ordered to report to a new company and told to stand on a given billet number marked on the floor. Chief Nicks, who resembled Hank Williams in stature and facial profile, stood in front looking us over. Chief Nicks called out my number and told me to come up front.

"Recruit Thomas Earl Harrawood, you are going to be my RCPO of Company 257." I didn't know what being an RCPO entailed, but my new Company Commander filled me in. I would "be him" when he was not around. I was a recruit Chief Petty Officer. I gave the orders, called the cadence, and got the company of eighty recruits to the drills on the grinder. I got them to the classes on time. I marched them to the mess hall. I also detailed my Recruit Master at Arms to assign "bright work" duty or to "clean the heads." I was the Inspecting Officer before we were given an inspection. I was their leader. But, of course, I would learn all this just as the others learned their duties.

Chief Nicks handed me a clipboard with the roster and told me to read out the names. I spoke low to him, "Sir, I can't read." Chief Nicks called the yeoman up front. He instructed him to read, and for the rest of boot camp I gave the orders but my yeoman read out the names or any special instructions that were written out. I found out that if someone could be my reader, I could facilitate the required leadership needed to fulfill the mission. It was an awesome bit of responsibility, and there were those who on occasion challenged me. One such case involved a big bull of a guy from Kansas.

I made sure that I was fair in ordering men to "turn to" and not having them do the same task over, at least not back to back. It was the first time I asked "Kansas" to clean heads, and I was challenged by him. I had my own office and invited him to step inside—and damn if he didn't. Inside he picked up a Navy coffee mug, which was a big, heavy ceramic cup without a handle. The mug could have been used for a soup bowl, but Kansas used it to smash in my nose. Blood was streaming down my face, but I somehow got a finger on the inside corner of his mouth and made a scratch, drawing some blood. Members of the company came rushing in and separated us. "Okay you Kansas son-of-a-bitch, if you want any more of that just come on back," I said, challenging him with tearing eyes and spitting blood. In spite of my busted-up nose, I won, because Old Kansas was by far the biggest guy in 257; everyone now knew that I would stand my command ground, regardless of the circumstances.

Chief Nicks confronted me the next morning and asked, "RCPO, did you have an accident?"

"Yes sir, I wolled out ob my bunk and hit mah wocker," I said, trying my best to communicate with blackened eyes, swollen lips and tongue, and a busted-up nose.

"RCPO, did everything work out okay?" Chief Nicks inquired.

"Yes sir, ebery tang is allraat."

By and large we were a harmonized company of "Blue Jackets." There was just one other instance that created a bit of a rub between the rest of 257 and me. It was about 0200 hour when Chief Nicks came in one evening with whiskey on his breath and shook me up out of sleep. He ordered me to get the company out on the grinder in fifteen minutes. I turned the lights on, but was dressed down because lights were not supposed to come on after we were given the "lights out" command.

Now, the standard uniform for us while doing infantry drills included dungarees, a pistol belt around the waist, and the WWII M1 Garand rifle. This uniform was used in physical training, infantry drills, and our 16-count manual exercises. But the RCPO carried the naval saber with scabbard. One military exercise that we practiced was called the "five and dive." When the command was given, the RCPO went from attention to a parade rest position. The sailors in the company would bend over with the rifle butt resting on the ground. The rifle would then be put in an upright position, resting against the left leg and leaning slightly outward. Simultaneously, the recruit would make a deep forward bend, and with both hands reach up and grab each side of his cover (hat). In normal circumstances we practiced this drill with music, and a fifth heavy drum beat would signify the moment of doing this exercise … in normal training that is. But that night, Chief gave the command "Fifth heavy drum beat readeeeee… TWO ! Every one performed as they were trained, but without the rifles. For me, however, he gave the order to draw my scabbard and to smack the rears of the recruits he named out.

I smacked the first one lightly, but then Chief said, "RCPO, you smack 'em hard or I'll smack you."

WHACK! I heard a whispering tone from the prey ... "Harrawood, I'll get you tomorrow!" Thankfully the wee-hour exercise was terminated after only a few ass whacks.

One day, I was put in for an honor award called "Outstanding Recruit," and it could only have been Chief Nicks that nominated me. I stood before three Officers who questioned me on the chain of command—from President Eisenhower on down—and specific military questions. One Officer asked me about my GCT score of 72. He called Chief Nicks in and asked him, "Did you know that the RCPO has a 72 GCT?"

Chief Nicks replied, "No sir, I did not know that. But sir, he has been one of my finest, if not the best, RCPO I have worked with."

Having a GCT of 72 enabled me, at any time I wished, to leave the Navy with an honorable discharge. I had my ups and downs, but I would prove to be a good "Blue Jacket."

The committee denied me the award, but Chief Nicks' support for me was worth all the medals or awards on the entire base. There were a few more boot camp incidents, but for nine weeks and five days I marched to the side of a group of prior civilians who were diverse in countless ways. I led my shipmates until graduation day.

The blue company guidon with gold numbers flapped in the San Diego breeze, and the orders for the Brigade to "REEE-PORT" was given. I stood at attention with my saber resting upright against my right arm and bellowed out, "COMPANY TWO FIFTY-SEVEN PRESENT AND ACCOUNTED FOR, SIR." The band struck up, and the brigade began "Passing in Review." Seaman Apprentice Thomas Earl Harrawood, a true "White Hat," was ready for official United States Navy orders.

Seventh Fleet

I requested orders to serve with Ed on the USS Estes AGC 12, Amphibious Force Flagship. AGCs are named after mountains or mountain ranges. The Estes was the twelfth ship in the Mount McKinley class. This ship was designed to serve as a floating headquarters and communications center. Various Commanders execute their amphibious assaults from such ships. The Estes was commissioned in 1944 and served at Iwo Jima and Okinawa, where it transported UDT teams to the Japanese islands. This was just one of the many distinguished missions that our ship performed in the Seventh Fleet.

Ed, Doris, their son Kevin, and I all lived for a short time together in an apartment not too far from our ship. I bought a little motor scooter, and we rode double, back and forth to the ship. It was during these days that this little band of Harrawoods took some 'R and R' (rest and recuperation). Once we made a long weekend trip up the coast line to Disneyland, where we saw a crowd gathering around a speaker. We meandered over and saw a young Bobby Kennedy campaigning for his brother, John Fitzgerald, who was vying for president.

After R and R, we were back in San Diego packing up. Doris and Kevin returned to the east. Ed and I went back to the Estes.

The first and only time Ed and I "steamed" together was on the Estes. The order to "Up Anchor" was given, and the USS Estes was underway for a West Pacific tour.

It was nice being on an Admiral's flagship, as it received a lot of special attention, visiting the best ports and providing beneficial perks for the crew. On the other hand, a flagship was expected to have a squared away crew and vessel. The Master Chief Boatswain Mate kept us busy doing brightwork. We chipped or slapped on Measure 13 Battleship Grey paint (or as every sailor knew it, Haze Grey).

Early on in the cruise I was often the butt of jokes on the Estes, not for any reasons other than I was the new deck ape. When ordered by a senior to go get a bucket of steam, I asked, "Okay, where do I get that?" I was told to go find out myself. I'd go from compartment to compartment before I eventually got smart. I might be sent for ten feet of Irish pennants. Another time a senior gave me orders to get in my dress blues, stand at the aft gun, and be on the lookout for a tugboat. So there I stood, in my Navy blues, like an idiot, watching for a tug that would never arrive while all the other mates were in their work dungarees. It was good seamanship being played on this striker.

A striker is the term for an enlisted man in training for a particular rating. I was striking for Boatswain's Mate. Having two diagonal stripes on my sleeve indicated that I was an E-2, a Seaman Apprentice (SA). Being just a Seaman Apprentice, I was not to have the Boatswain rating symbol of crossed anchors on my sleeve; this was reserved as an overall rating of Petty Officers, E-4 through E-9. For the duration of this tour I was assigned to keep the compartment, lines, rigging, and deck machinery in shipshape condition. I held a variety of positions such as lookout, helmsman, and fire sentry, and I was a member of the security and gun crews.

The cruise took us to the Far East where the ships docked at Yokosuka, Japan. We were involved in various amphibious operations in the waters surrounding the Philippines, Okinawa, and Korea. We steamed all over the South China Sea, Yellow Sea, Sea of Japan, and the Philippine Sea. We participated in exercises with the Royal Navy, the Royal Navy New Zealand, and Korea. On shore liberty, as might be expected, Ed and I immersed ourselves in typical sailor "adventures," staying clear of Shore Patrol. In Hong Kong I bought a fancy Hong Kong Shark Skin tailored suit with a matching vest, and two sets of china. I gave one to my sister, Lois

Ann, and one to Mom.

One might think that a sailor gets bored; however, certainly not a deck ape and especially not one on a flagship. I was always busy and always got the job done. When told "turn to," my superiors knew it would be done right, proficiently and the Navy Way. Those who didn't do it right suffered the consequences.

The ship was moored at Manila Bay. A strict warning was given when going ashore, "Do not drink the Manila rum!" But there's always at least one. This one we called Andy. Andy was least liked among us deck apes. He was what we called a "sea lawyer," or an enlisted man who likes to argue; usually one who thinks he can twist the regulations and standing orders around to favor his personal inclinations. I was on the ship attending the eight o'clock movie when I heard a commotion on the quarterdeck. It was a very saturated Manila-rummed Andy. He was fighting the Officer of the Deck (OOD) and completely out of his pea-sized brain. Some crewmen and I held him down and strapped him to a stretcher. They were carrying him up the ladder to sick bay when the XO looked over the railing, and Andy spit in his face. The last time I saw Andy, his hat was pulled down over his eyes and he was doing the "Brig Shuffle," with two big guards escorting him through the chow hall. Lesson: Follow ship's orders.

I quickly reached a high point on my first tour. The crew of the USS Estes cheered at the hoisting of the Homeward Bound Pennant. This flag, the most colorful of flags, is flown by a ship that has been on overseas duty continuously for nine months or more and is headed back home to the States. Once the flag is flown for twenty-four hours in the States, it is brought down. The blue portion of the flag is given to the captain, and the rest is cut up into sections and given to the crew members. Ed and I were ready to get back stateside, with or without a piece of flag.

Ed had finished his "kiddie tour." A kiddie tour is when you come in at seventeen years old, but you get out on your twenty-first birthday. Ed headed back east to Missouri, and I headed back out to sea on the Estes.

In early 1962, around my twentieth birthday, a request was made across the fleet for Assault Boat Coxswain (ABC) volunteers, and I submitted my request for the duty. At the same time my ship left San Diego and commenced operations in the Pacific Northwest. This was the Estes' second trip up the coast. We moored in Seattle during the opening of the World's Fair, and I took the time to go up the Space Needle. I was glad I did because my shipmates and I met some fun-loving girls.

I received orders in San Diego to attend Assault Boat Coxswain (ABC) School in Coronado. ABC school was held during the day so after class I returned across the bay to the ship. The instructors made note that I was a natural. For me, handling a boat was simply mechanical. I learned to judge distance years ago by steering tractors that pulled wagons close to the hay bales, or backing manure spreaders alongside of barns and into barn slots. I had learned to maintain a steady hand on the blade lever of a bulldozer, while balancing the right amount of throttle to most efficiently push material for a distance. In other words, I learned years ago how to "read" a boat.

Later I was standing for the ship's personnel inspection. The Captain of the ship, scrutinizing the rank of sailors, came up to me face to face. The captain asked in a forthright way, "Harrawood, didn't you put in a request for the LST Force?"

"Yes sir, Captain, a couple months or so back, Captain," I explained.

The Captain looked over to the XO, and in a curt command asked, "Why hasn't Harrawood been sent? They're badly in need of boat coxswains over there."

When a four-striped Captain speaks, it is seldom ignored. I was told to pack my seabag and given a thirty-day leave because I would be going overseas for two years' duty. The Captain said they really needed boatmen over there badly because, quite simply, as a future president might have said, "our long nightmare" in Southeast Asia was just beginning.

My enthusiasm in fulfilling my duties aboard the Estes did not go unobserved, and I received a fair amount of gratitude from those whose opinions I valued the most. I made good friends that still live in my memory's sea chest, and the Bo'sun of the deck wished me well when I departed as a full E-3 Seaman (SN) and a genuine salty Blue Jacket. In two days I was off the Estes and driving back to Missouri in an old 1948 Ford I bought from a good shipmate of mine.

LST 1166 Washtenaw County

After a whirlwind leave home, I gave the keys of the '48 Ford to Ed, and before all the tears were dried from my mother's eyes, I headed back to the West Coast.

My orders sent me first to Los Angeles International to board a flight to Clark Air Base in Manila. I boarded my flight for Manila via Honolulu. For two weeks I was in transit at Clark Air Base, and from there they sent me to Yokosuka by air where I reported for duty on the 1166 LST Washtenaw County.

LSTs (or Tank Landing Ships) derive their names from counties of the United States. Of all the amphibious ships, these are conceivably the most familiar on the seas. These ships are designed with a shallow draft so they can be driven onto a beach to unload tanks and other assault vehicles. The vehicles or tanks drive over a ramp through doors that open horizontally at its bow. On the inside a ramp exists that enables tanks to get from top deck down to the tank deck. The Washtenaw County carried

16 Officers and 189 Enlisted. She was 384 feet in length with a beam of 55 feet. She was capable of 14 knots.

Not long after I boarded the LST 1166 and established my pecking order, I was made the Leading Seaman. While not an official U.S. Navy title, a Leading Seaman is, nonetheless, acknowledged by everyone as the "don't take no lip" guy, and in seafaring days of the tall ships it meant you pretty much were required to kick any other "crackerjack's" ass on the ship. But it was my sense of humor, my boat-handling abilities, and the ABC patch on my shoulder that led the Chief Bo'sun to make me the LST Leading Seaman.

As the Coxswain, pronounced "koksun," I was placed in charge of a boat. I was usually Helmsman, the man who steers the boat. The boats I normally worked with were small landing crafts, and I was responsible for the Landing Crafts (LC). There were as many uses for LCs as there were boats. These crafts were usually identified by their abbreviation. For example: LCM would be identified as landing craft, mechanized; LCVP, vehicle and personnel; LCP (L), personnel, large; and LCP(R), personnel, ramp. My favorite duty was the Captain gigs.

Captain gigs are boats used by Commanding Officers and Chiefs of Staff that are not flag rank. The 36-foot LCP (L) is a normal boat, but different only from other LCs in that it has a canopy, usually canvas. The Captain's boat usually had a few chrome fittings on the hull and interior, and to know for sure if the Captain is aboard, his personal flag was on the bow.

Another boat that I operated was an LCM-6 known as a "Mike Boat." This boat was a porcupine in that was heavily armed and used as an early assault and insertion craft for Army advisors and SEAL personnel. These Mike Boats were nicknamed "Mighty Mo." The SEALs (SeaAir-Land) teams were newly commissioned out of the UDTs. A call across the fleet for volunteers was made, and I really thought of volunteering but was pretty sure that my inability to read or write would restrict me.

Military Assistance Command (MACV) had been funneling aid to South Vietnam as early as 1955, and by the time I appeared in Southeast Asia, the new President Kennedy was already escalating the effort to stave off communist aggression in this part of the world. This fired up the Southeast Asian Treaty Organization (SEATO) allies, and every country that had interest in that area, especially the Philippines, New Zealand, and Australia. The white numbers of 1166 could be found beached at Pohang, South Korea. It could be seen with ramps down delivering armored vehicles, construction equipment or Marines at Danang, China Beach, and Saigon, South Vietnam. We were also in the coastal waters of Borneo, working in its jungle rivers, cross-training, or training inshore maritime operations known as Brown Water Ops. Sometimes we were moored, waiting to be loaded with equipment in Subic Bay, P.I., or even at our home port in Yokosuka, Japan. I operated boats at many places that eventually all looked the same.

Once our LST 1166 was beached with its ramp down offloading Marines in their armored amphibian tractors (AmTrac). I was on the beach when a battery exploded on an AmTrac, badly burning a Marine. I administered to his wounds the best I could. The poor boy had his eyes burned completely out. A helicopter was coming in to pick him up, and I leaned over him to shield him from the rotary wash. When the Corpsman lifted him onto the stretcher, he died. I believe it may have been a blessing for him.

One time I was badly hurt while operating the Captain's gig. The 1166 was anchored out, and I came in with the boat to pick up the sea painter (a fixed line connected to the ship). My bowhook man must secure the line to a cleat on the bow of my boat. When this line is secure, I go to reverse, "back down on the painter" to hold the boat up against the gangway. A combination of events set the stage for the accident: First, the tide rushed out; then the sea painter line snapped; and finally, the particular engines on this boat were known to fail when the helmsman went from reverse to forward quickly. My boat was in the backward motion when the engines failed, and the tide pushed my boat in under the waterline of the ship. I tried to protect my boat by jumping up on the canopy and pushing off the ship but I was slammed into the steel giant, smashing my legs. The boat then swung out free of the ship with other crewmen, getting it quickly secured. Crumbled up in the boat and in excruciating pain, a couple of Corpsmen jumped aboard and started treating me. I began chilling and drifting into shock from the way they had my legs hanging over the canopy. I really got teed off when the Corpsman cut off my new dungarees.

    I was loaded up in another boat and shoved off for shore where I was given a shot of morphine in a field medical unit. I was not marked, indicating a morphine shot was given, but until I passed out I was being strangely amused by the geckos darting about on the tent walls. I was on a gurney when I came to the next morning.

    A Second Class Corpsman was looking me over. I asked him if I could get some chow. "Can't do because the mess is closing down," he told me in a gruff response.

    I was in luck because an old Chief Warrant Officer Boatswain Mate, one of the "gods of the Navy," was walking by and saw the ABC patch on my uniform. "How you doing Boats? What happened to you?"

    I commenced telling him about my accident and that I was hungry. He asked the Corpsman why I couldn't get chow. That's when "god" let the PO2 Corpsman have both barrels. "This sailor's out there on the water all the time while you sit on your rear-end dry docked," he said and then turned to me, "Can you get in a wheel chair, Boats?"

"Yes sir, I believe I can." I replied. Then he made the Corpsman push me down to the mess hall. The mess gang was just cleaning up the breakfast detail when we came rolling in. The Warrant Officer asked the galley crew in a commanding way to fix me up some breakfast. And since they weren't going to say no, they fixed me breakfast. The Warrant and I talked while I ate, but then he left me with a bad-tempered Second Class. When that Corpsman gave my next shot, it felt like he was using a jack hammer with a square needle.

I had another incident as Helmsman on the Captain's gig that happened when we were approaching the gangway. The Captain, a Lieutenant Commander who I really liked, asked me, "Harrawood, can I land the gig?"

To that I replied, "It's your boat Capt'n."

The Captain took the helm and was coming in too fast, gunning it up while turning in the wrong way. The boat slammed hard into the gangway. The OOD looked over and asked in a not-so-pleasing way what was going on. The Captain said, "Harrawood, you take the blame for this, please. If you do take the blame, when we get back to Yokosuka, I'll have this boat worked over real nice."

"Aye Aye Capt'n." As if I was going to tell him otherwise. But boy did I get chewed out from my Chief Boatswain Mate for coming in hot. So I guess I was an unsung Navy hero for the Captain.

One of my maritime achievements was being a marksman for the LST. During Director School I was firing three-inch/50s at a target screen being pulled by a tug. The guns were either computer-controlled or manual-controlled, and I was supposed to shoot manually. I was firing at the targets, blam … blam … blam! when the Captain walked over and shouted down at the crew, "My god! That's good shooting. Darn good, Harrawood!" The gunner's mate came over to me and said, "Don't you ever tell anybody that we were locked on, Harrawood. Okay I'll take the credit.

LST 1166 steamed into Hong Kong, and I went on liberty with a heavily tattooed sailor. He wanted to get a tattoo of the middle finger on the bottom of his big toe so when he was lying in his rack he'd be giving every one the finger. I had no plans whatsoever of getting a tattoo, but while he was getting "inked up," I was browsing through the catalog of potential themes. I saw one that was clever: a wood pecker with wood chips flying out of my butt. Another one was a skunk holding his nose, and this would be in the same locale as the wood pecker. I thought about it and decided I didn't want that Chinese guy with an ink gun back there on my ass. But I did get a Dennis the Menace look alike and his girlfriend imprinted on the top of my feet. It was supposed to be Dennis on the right foot saying "Hi Baby" and his girl on the left foot replying "Who Me." I'm not so sure what happened, but the tattoo artist inked it in as "Who Baby" and "Hi Me."

War games and ships' security were always being tested while in port. One particular day was counter sabotage day. A dummy bomb was hidden or smuggled onboard a ship by a sailor from another ship. It was a game of high stakes because it meant the ship that detected their bomb or intercepted the saboteur earned the coveted "E" for efficiency.

I was selected by the Bo'sun to smuggle a bomb onto our rival ship. Our bomb would be concealed as batteries for a battle lantern, which must be acknowledged by the "referees." So I nonchalantly walked down the pier to our target ship and up to the quarter deck.

"Request permission to come aboard," I asked in a 'just another day on the job' way. "I need some new batteries ... we got a detail down in the bilges." This was a typical sprinkling of regular ship talk to the watch.

The watch motioned for the messenger of the watch to take me down to the electrical room. I stacked my bomb batteries up against the magazine bulkhead and with the replacements headed back up topside.

"Permission to leave ship?"

When I got back down on the pier, the referees came out and informed the watch that they've "been bombed."

"What'ya mean we've been bombed?" the OOD asked. The refs brought me up, and we all went back down to the electrical room where I showed them the bomb. "Well you a##%&*@." They didn't get the big "E."

I was on the morning watch from 0400 hour to 0800 hour on November 23, 1963, but in Dallas, Texas, it was the 22nd. On that watch you call reveille. The messenger of the watch read to me that President Kennedy had been shot. I broadcast this over the microphone, and immediately people came up to me and asked to repeat what I said. I do not recall going to General Quarters; that's something you would remember. I do remember the ship's company was given four days to mourn the death of our Commander in Chief. Most of us hit the bars to drown our sorrows.

Another key moment was when General Quarters was sounded, which is an announcement to signal that all hands aboard a ship must go to battle stations as quickly as possible. We heard it on March 28, when a great earthquake, magnitude 9.2, struck the Prince William Sound region of Alaska, shaking the earth for four and a half minutes. A tsunami warning went out to all the fleet in this area; but, if there was a wave we never felt it, and it came to nothing.

One sunny tropical afternoon, the Chief Boatswain Mate struck up a conversation with me about my Navy career. He told me I was a squared-away seaman for my outstanding work and exemplary Navy attitude. Then he asked why I wasn't an E-4 yet. I explained that I just wasn't able to read or write on the test.

The test is given fleet wide on the same date, and you are competing against every seaman of your rate. When it came time to take the test, the Chief Boatswain Mate and a lieutenant sat next to me while I took the test. It was a multiple choice test, and as I went down the page I'd use my pencil to point to the answers. The Chief would clear his throat, sounding something like he was saying "uh uh" and then clear his throat again when my pencil hit the right answer. They took the test for me.

Finally, in May of 1964, I decided to put in for my discharge. The Chief asked me why, and I explained to him that he would not be there to help me again for the E-5 exam, or the E-6, or the chief's exam in twelve years or more.

I boarded a military flight in Japan via Anchorage, Alaska, and flew back to the Naval base at Treasure Island, San Francisco. I had to eat up a few remaining weeks in transit, then on June 9, 1964, I began hitchhiking east, for the last time.

My days steaming on the USS Estes AGC 12 and on the 1166 LST Washtenaw County proved to me that, though I was handicapped with a learning disability, my disability was with the written language, nothing else. When details were read to me, I executed them to the minutest detail. I was not able to decipher the written word, but I could listen. And when life and death matters were at hand, I clamped on to every word of instruction and gained the confidence of my superiors that those directions would be carried out to their fullest meaning. If anything, thus far, I came to understand this about me. I realized I must be keen and sharp in developing listening and observation skills—to read a man when he was speaking to me. I respected the words of men with experience as opposed to those who held an arrogant attitude over me. And as Ike Eisenhower said "An intellectual is a man who takes more words than necessary to tell more than he knows." It was one of the main lessons learned in the Navy—clear commands, the Navy Way.

A ship that is disabled or uncontrollable in the Navy is referred to as "not under command." Was I disabled? Uncontrollable? No! I'm in command of this vessel called Tom.

Back Words

CHAPTER TEN

A Darn Fool

One good thing about being a seaman, and a single one at that, is the carefree life that it affords. No anxiety over medical insurance, no concerns about seeking dental care, no worry about having to set appointments for various services, and no frets over salary. The Navy always paid me. Finally, no need to be bothered about where the next meal comes from; it was always provided whether I was broke or not. I sold back Navy leave days and, with a few sea dollars saved up, I was provided short-term security. For all the safekeeping that I left behind in the Fleet, I was well aware that I would be the sole provider for Tom Harrawood here on out. I also knew that I could always find a bunk at Mom and Frank's house. From Bridgeton, Missouri, my parents moved across the "Big Muddy" Mississippi River, and now lived in Godfrey, Illinois.

That's where Bridges Paving had their asphalt plant. It operated just across the road from a house trailer that my parents had rented. Frank had worked himself up to a full supervisor for Bridges. He was now overseeing the paving aspect of the near-thirty-mile link of the Great River Road, which would be called the "Meeting of the Great Rivers Scenic Byway."

This paving job paralleled the Mississippi. It began just a few miles upriver from Alton, Illinois, and ended at Grafton, Illinois, where the Illinois River emptied into the Mississippi. I was certain that I could become gainfully employed by Bridges Paving since Frank was a super, Gayle was a foreman, and Ed worked for Gayle. Jim was working for Frank at the Godfrey asphalt plant.

I began stretching out my civilian muscles by buying a very used Chevrolet Corvair. (Shortly after I bought this automobile it had the distinction of being one of the products with "designed-in-dangers" that consumer advocate Ralph Nader uncovered in his exposition, "Unsafe at any Speed.") Transportation secured, I needed to find a job. The job, as might be expected, came from Bridges through my brother Gayle.

There might have been chinks in the Harrawood armor, but when a Harrawood man vouched for another Harrawood man, there was a code of honor, a sense of obligation, and a sense of duty to not only perform, but to be better than your peers. Frank may have passed down to us boys some sort of dysfunctional ability in interpreting the written language, but this, sure as heck, is a fact: The fabric of a ferocious work ethic cloaked us, and our employers recognized it. Gayle understood the code and knew that I would be grateful for the employment opportunity. And now I worked with Gayle and Ed, my seniors, just like we were back there in the old Hoosier land.

Gayle was foreman at a small asphalt plant located in Peerless Park, Missouri. The plant was fifty miles from my parents' home, but seemed farther when driving in my unsafe-at-any-speed car. Skirting the bustling St. Louis suburbia made for a long day of driving. After two weeks and the end of my parents' welcome stay, I moved in with Gayle for a few months until I neared the expiration date on my hospitality card, then I moved in with Ed. Funny, but here, too, the welcome home embrace soon became a "get your own place" suggestion. I was able to find a home just a couple miles east of Peerless Park. It was an old-style auto court, sagging from time (to say the least), with individual cabins very similar to those that we occupied during our 1952 California trip. In fact, it was on old Route 66, the same road we traveled on our trip.

Across the road from my home was the new Chrysler plant, which was in the process of expanding. Chrysler was there because there was room. Growth was happening all over the western fringes of St. Louis County and especially along the westward path of the beginning interstate system, I-70. If you use my analogy of greater St. Louis being the left side of a clock, the Chrysler plant and Peerless Park, where I worked, were at the eight o'clock position. Open space lay between work and the old suburban edges of the city. Indeed, small farms and horse ranches existed, but certainly they were smack in front of an oncoming tsunami of progress. The St. Louis population in 1960 was 750,026; ten years later, in 1970, it was 622,236. Close to 130 thousand folks migrated westward from the city to surrounding communities, expanding the St. Louis metropolitan area as well as creating the designation "West County." Opportunity presented itself like low-hanging fruit for anyone who was bold enough to pick it.

I was able to watch the old Mother Road, US-66, being gobbled up right before my eyes by a new conduit coming out of St. Louis: Interstate 44. The Peerless Park Asphalt Plant, as it was known, was located at the intersection of Missouri State 141 and the developing Federal I-44. The one-and-a-half-ton batch plant provided asphalt for various requirements called for on the I-44 project. The orders for I-44 kept the plant busy because the asphalt plant was only capable of producing a mere five hundred tons a day. My responsibility was to operate a bulldozer and keep the stock piles heaped up near the cold materials bin. Otherwise, I worked with Ed on the plant as an operator, keeping the assorted bearings, elevator chains, levers and supporting equipment lubricated. You might say that I was the acting "deck ape" at the plant.

On one occasion a request was posed to me, "Tom, can you operate a paver?" (In the construction business, and especially in earthmoving and the paving arena, only a rookie would say "I can run" a piece of machinery. A Harrawood would say "I can operate it." So that's what I did. I quickly examined the mechanism, checked the oil, looked it over, and mounted it like I'd been riding this horse forever.

I had never been on a paving machine. It was an ancient chain-driven, lever-operated Barber Greene paver. As I sat on it, I looked out at the site and could see crushed stone being spread as a base. I can shorten this story by just saying that the laborers using their hand tools had no praise for me as they filled in the lows and knocked off the highs left behind by this paving operator.

Working for big brother Gayle presented an added bonus of being assigned the overtime that Ed and I really coveted. However, there was one little stipulation: to get this overtime we had to pay half of it to Gayle. That meant half of Ed's and half of my overtime went to Gayle who was on salary and now making as much as Ed and I made together. Ed and I figured half was better than none!

It was down in a pit at the asphalt plant that I had an epiphany that would forever be the basis of one of my life's mottos. I was cleaning out the spill that collected from the conveyers that moved the cold materials onto the mixing drum. A well-dressed man exited from his Oldsmobile, and, in a very confident and controlled manner, walked around the plant and over to where another worker and I were busy tossing out the tailings. He looked down on us for a few moments, and we made eye contact. No conversation was struck up, and just as quickly as he came, he got back in his car and drove off. "Who was that guy?" I asked my co-worker.

"Why that was Mr. Bridges himself. He owns this plant," my co-worker replied.

I was smacked in the head by a certain reality: *If Mr. Bridges can work me and make a profit off of my labor, why can't I work me and make a profit off of myself?*

One day a fellow came into the plant and asked if we did patch work. I made a call downtown and was informed that these kinds of jobs were too small for the company to deal with. Ding…ding! The opportunity bell sounded off in my head. I quickly asked if the company would mind if Ed and I took the job. The answer was that they didn't mind, but we would have to buy Bridge's asphalt.

Ed and I gathered up an assortment of tools we suspected would be needed. We obtained a truck from just down the road at Valley Mount Horse Ranch to carry the asphalt. We were friends with the owners, who were down-to-earth, hardworking people and who reminded us of the kind of people we had known back in Indiana.

The plan developed like this: We found the trailer court where we were to repair the patch work; guessed as to how much material we would need; estimated how much time we thought it would take; and set a date for the job.

Our regular job started at 7:00 am and ended at 3:30 pm. Since Ed and I were the ones who normally made the asphalt, we made our own, and it was understood that we were to safely secure the plant afterward. We made two tons on the nose, dropped the batch of asphalt in the old Valley Mount truck, and I drove it to the job. Ed followed in a pickup with the tools, including a hand-pulled roller. Ed and I were well versed in how to make the asphalt, but not so keen on putting it down. But, boy did we learn things quickly, like spraying down our truck bed and tools with a light coating of diesel fuel so the asphalt doesn't stick to the metal, and not standing on hot asphalt for too long. Nonetheless, our very first job took us three hours, and we were paid $90.00. Asphalt was $3.75 per ton times two, which was $7.50 plus $1.00 for gas. Our expenses came to $8.50. Subtract that from our $90.00, and we made a profit of $81.50. Split that, and

I made just over $13.00 per hour. I made $3.00 per hour at my regular job. Immediately, Ed and I began scouring for more jobs and equipment. Gayle was indifferent to our side jobs at first, until he realized the extra money we were making and required a kickback.

We found a little one-ton roller without an engine over in East St. Louis, and we bought a used 8hp Briggs and Stratton engine that we worked over. The darn Briggs was started by a pulley rope, and everyone eventually ended up with a busted up arm or scraped knuckles from its compression kickback. But we had ourselves a roller. Next, we found an old trailer hidden by weeds. We acquired it, put new tires all around, repacked bearings, and gave it a good overhaul. It wasn't too long before one job led to another, sometimes just across from the job we were doing. Ed and I just kept returning our profits into assets, which allowed us to take on bigger jobs. I felt there was enough fruit for me to pick alone, so I struck out on my own. The irony of this was that while Ed and I were building up a business, Bridges Paving was in the process of closing down. At this point in my life I made my first official partnership.

In the fall of 1965 I married Sue Seeley, a High Ridge, Missouri, girl. We began our home life in a small but comfortable home in Manchester. Sue and I would later become the parents of two daughters, Stephanie and Robin, and our son, Chris. After this momentous resolution to build a family, I made my next big decision.

The summer of 1966 I left Bridges and received Frank's typical blessing: "You are a darn fool." Gayle went to work for Fred Weber, a construction and quarry company, and Ed stayed on with Bridges for another year. But after his regular work hours, Ed would help me on the jobs we acquired. We never looked back.

Chapter 10 - A Darn Fool

Show Me

In the infancy of our enterprise, an opportunity presented itself in the form of a paint spray gun. A customer wanted a ramp asphalted that led down to the lower level of a two-story building. The building was used to spray paint metal alphabetic letters in a six-inch font for interchangeable messages on advertising signs. The man we were paving the ramp for sub-contracted from a business in St. Louis. In passing conversation he mentioned he was looking for someone to help paint the letters. I didn't hesitate in presenting myself as a potential painter, explaining that I had experience painting with spray guns in the Navy. We began spray painting in the evening, and soon after the sub-contractor offered the business to us. Gayle, Ed, and I talked it over, accepted the offer, and were introduced to the owner of the mother company. A contract was made and, for a short time, we worked out of the sub-contractor's shop.

It was approximately the same time that a building with a separate multi-bay garage became available in Manchester on Highway 100. We acquired the building by signing a lease and moved the paint operation there. The Harrawood men now had a base of operations; a place where we could maintain our equipment, make needed repairs, store our tools, and paint the fonts. I could honestly say that I was finally a man of letters.

These painted letters were in the day-glow colors of lime, red, and orange. In the evening the wives of Gayle and Ed would remove the letters from the drying racks and pack the letters in their corrugated cardboard boxes for delivery. Eventually, we laid out a sort of production line. This painting contract resulted in an excellent cash flow for us.

Our inventory increased by obtaining two International trucks with stake beds that we outfitted with fuel tanks and tool racks. Ed and I were elated by how well these Internationals performed. We claimed that we often had to stop and siphon gas out of the tanks because they made gas and overflowed.

Now I was painting, prospecting for jobs, and doing the jobs with Ed and Gayle after their regular working hours. Then we landed a job at a shopping mall in Ballwin, Missouri, which further bolstered our confidence and self-reliance. For Ed, this was when he made the decision to leave Bridges Paving and work full time in our efforts. The estimation on the parking lot required us to place fifty-two tons of asphalt. We hired locals, and in one day, using only hand tools, we accomplished the job with a net profit of $1,000. The amount of opportunities that were opening up in West County now demanded that we hire a full-time man.

Mike Swartz was that man. We put him on letter-painting full time, but he worked in the field whenever needed. Mike had a thick head of blonde hair parted very distinctly. When he spoke, he slobbered slightly. And his right eye was slow with a drooping eyelid. He could have played any part in a war movie as a German soldier. Mike was a loyal man and never wavered during good or bad times.

During this time, Gayle was released from Fred Weber's company because he had a hernia, and now all three of us were fully engaged in our company. Gayle was never much of a field man, so in the early days he and his wife, Darlene, worked the paint shop and oversaw paperwork.

At the beginning of our infant company, there were many things that required my full attention and concentration. For instance, a potential customer once asked me how many square yards of asphalt would be needed for a job.

Square yards?

I reported back to the brothers that we had a possible job, but he wants to know how many square yards would be needed. That night the three of us taught ourselves how to find square feet and yards, and how to multiply the square yardage depending on the asphalt depth. We developed a scale so Ed and I could do basic estimations (one ton of asphalt covered nine square yards at two inches). This may seem elementary, and it was, but not for me. Words and symbols were not the same for me as they were for someone without dyslexia. Nevertheless, if instructions were read out and demonstrated once, that's all I needed.

Another instance that demonstrated just how much we were learning in those early days was a job we encountered on Lindbergh Road. We were paving a parking lot for a building contractor, Clark Park, who was an engineer and supervised the job sites for the company he worked for. After I roughed out the basic grade Mr. Park asked me, "Will it drain off?"

"Yes, sure it will," I responded.

"How do you know?" Mr. Park was quick to ask.

"Well, I can see that it will," I answered, in a less-than-positive tone.

"Do you have a transit?" he asked.

"A what?" I answered, trying to hold back my growing frustration.

"A transit and level; look, you bring a level and grade rod back tomorrow," he said.

That night I went to Sears and Roebuck and bought a grade rod, a level transit, and a tripod. This was very intimidating equipment for me, but Mr. Park took the mystery out of it. Very methodically he taught me how to set and level the transit, and then he taught me how to read the rod.

"See, now when the numbers go down," he elaborated, "the grade is going up. And when the numbers go up, the grade is going down." Mr. Park, a very patient instructor, worked with me the rest of the day. Only when he was sure that I understood these tools and how to use them did he cut me loose. Mr. Park was a pure gentleman and a valued mentor. Moreover, he supplied us with lots of work from then on, so much so, that it helped fortify the Harrawood brothers' venture. I became so adept at using these tools that, in later years, I instructed a class on their application. And, by the way, had it not been for Mr. Park, there would have been water puddles on that first job!

Another job providing a learning experience came from the Spirit of St. Louis Airport. The airport location was on the extreme northwest corner of St. Louis County, butting up to the Missouri River. New airplane hangars were being built, and we were asked to do the grade. I did not need my level and rod as the grade had already been staked out—not in inches, but in tenths of inches. Once again I swallowed my pride by opening up to the surveyor who initially laid out the job. He was an understanding man who uncomplainingly taught me how to translate in tenths. All my life the only measurement I knew was that twelve inches made a foot.

By this time the Harrawood boys were all in our business together, but it was a Massey-Ferguson tractor with a grader blade that sealed the partnership. The purchase of a grading tractor was well overdue for us, and we found one for fifteen hundred dollars. We came to an agreement after an evening meeting. Each of us would put up five hundred dollars for the tractor and if you didn't, then you were not coming in. We all came up with the money and bought the tractor. On that transaction, Harrawood Brothers Incorporated was born.

The Big Blue H

From our friends at Valley Mount Ranch we found a very efficient employee: Louise Lake. She was dark-haired and petite, with hints of Native American in her high cheek bones and alert dark eyes. Louise may have been small in stature, but she had a gigantic personality. She became our first official Office Manager. She had a lot of experience in bookkeeping and office savvy (though she had no formal training), and she kept us out of trouble. The perceptive Louise knew that the Harrawood brothers' handicap existed in reading and writing only. Her insightfulness created a trustworthy bond for all of us, and her competence provided an integral part of the now-evolving venture.

From the start, Louise made managing our business simple for us by creating, a "King Edward" filing system; also known as cigar boxes. We dropped our daily time-keeping receipts along with rock and asphalt tickets in the "in box." Another box was the "out box." Louise helped us in myriad ways, including finding potential jobs in newspapers, writing and sounding out clients' names, and in time helping us evaluate job estimates by interpreting and translating various aspects of bids and blueprints.

If such a thing as Asphalt Boatswain Mates existed, we found them in the Miller brothers. The Millers were big men out of the foothills of the Ozark Mountains, with bib overalls and handkerchiefs dangling out of hip pockets like rooster tails. They came swearing, cursing, tobacco-chewing, and spitting, but most of all they came ready to work. There were no others who knew how to put down asphalt like these brothers. Men like these, with their skills to read the highs and lows in spreading asphalt, were priceless for an emerging company like ours. The last thing you wanted after completing a job was hearing from the client that there were water puddles everywhere. The Millers passed on their asphalt-working skills to us.

We were growing, and Harrawood Brothers Inc., while maintaining the paint shop, moved south to a larger garage just across the Meramec River. We acquired an assortment of power tools, soil, sand, asphalt and aggregate, gas-powered plate compactors, walk-behind concrete saws, gas-powered tamping rammers, and an ever-growing assortment of necessary hand tools. A single axle Chevrolet dump truck was one of our earliest material-hauling trucks. If this old five-geared beast was loaded and going up a steep grade, it had to be in the lowest possible gear. While climbing a hill, the driver had to step out on the running board to escape the heat inside the cab. But a spreader box attached to the back of the truck enabled us to spread asphalt on driveways and parking lots more efficiently, and we quickly took on bigger jobs.

The Meramec River was notorious for its flooding, and we were not immune to an occasional deluge. We were flooded out in the first and only year that we were based there.

Eventually, Bridges asphalt plant at Peerless Park was sold to an Oklahoma contractor, and we helped to disassemble the plant. While doing so I looked down in the pit, where years earlier I had my encounter with Mr. Bridges, and I flashed on the thought that perhaps Mr. Bridges recognized himself down in that pit all those years ago. I smiled to myself on that reflection. We negotiated with our former employer to lease these grounds since Bridges Paving was defunct. This Peerless Park site became the new home of Harrawood Brothers Inc.

Next, we needed a logo. In the early years, we bought a three-quarter ton Chevy pickup as a crew support truck. It was a washed-out gold color, which we adopted as our company color—Harrawood Gold. We used this color and a big blue H with red edging as our logo. We were exceptionally proud of our color and of our equipment. Later we provided uniforms and baseball caps with the big blue H on the front, further giving our men a sense of belonging and pride in themselves and the company.

The way we maintained our equipment and kept it clean was instilled in our employees. The big H was quickly becoming recognized in the St. Louis area. We did not pay union scale, but the men we hired felt a kinship to us, and it was especially appreciated when Ed and I were both toiling alongside the men.

Brothers being brothers, though, Ed and I occasionally would get into heated arguments; a little falling-out usually over how to lay out a job, but mostly it was over nothing other than growing pains. Sometimes we even stepped back behind a building and slugged it out. But with the pressure released and the crack of a joke we all fell back in with our small family of a crew. That was just what we had developed into—a family—and these little squabbles meant nothing. The men also realized this.

However, a division was in the making, but one that enhanced the performance of the field work. I was more and more involved with the prep work for the paving—the dirt and rock man—and Ed became the asphalt man. Of course, we both worked at the entire business, but more and more the division of labor came down this way. I came to quickly assess requirements to make it easier for the finish. Ed knew what I needed to make his application smoother, so that in the end it really became a well-honed and synchronized operation. The upshot of this team effort brought an increase in profits and amplified the big blue H's quality, once again enabling us to take on more jobs. On the other end Gayle was widening his abilities to bid and acquire jobs and calculate the requirements, building up needed office logistics.

The physical base of our business was evolving, too. We got a job on Olive Street Road that required the removal of a large block building. We dismantled the building piece by piece, right up to the roof. Then the building was reconstructed at our base, giving us a very nice garage to work from. In addition, Gayle found a house trailer that we converted into an office, and it became Harrawood's 'front door.' A nice freshly painted block building, well-placed tool sheds, and Harrawood Gold-painted equipment sporting the big blue H parked in a semi-circle behind the office, told the construction community that a new kid was in town.

It was time to grow from strictly working in the private sector. Our eyes turned to landing government contracts: county, state, and federal. The bids for government jobs were being let out more and more, and we were poised and ready to reap the benefits of an economic expansion that would propel the company to its zenith.

Lyndon Baines Johnson was known as "Landslide Johnson" even before his massive rout of the Republican candidate, Barry Goldwater and his political party, in the 1964 presidential election. LBJ, as he preferred to be called, would initiate his Great Society programs. This impacted the Greater St. Louis area at exactly the same time that we were developing our company. Between Great Society dollars and our hard work, the possibility of obtaining a business loan enhanced our ability to grow.

Our first big-ticket item cost fifty thousand dollars. It was a brand new PF 500 Blaw-Knox paver that we purchased from Machinery Inc. in downtown St. Louis. Fifty thousand! This was a big leap for us, but Gayle, Ed, and I were resolute in making it happen because we never thought too much about what we could lose as much as what we could gain. Harrawood Brothers were just a few steps from "stepping out smartly."

The next move for the company was a solid bonding from a major insurance company that gave us enough tuck to bid on government jobs. To shore up the inside crew for Gayle and Louise, a Bridges Paving man came aboard the team.

Jim Spegal worked for Bridges Paving as an estimator and planner. Jim was as cordial a man as I've had the privilege to know. Course dark-hair, well-formed thick eyebrows, and just a little bit of a twist in the corner of his mouth when speaking only made his smile and laugh that more pleasant to view. Jim was the sort of man that when you struck up a conversation with him, he clung to every word you spoke, making you feel like you were the most important person in the world. Even just a sporty "Hi Jim, how are you?" and Jim's bold eyes and wide smile made you walk away with a better appreciation for the day. But behind the eyes of this very genial man was the seriousness of a grasshopper in a hen house. Jim worked the numbers, and his experience polished Harrawood Gold much more. Jim helped us bring in the first big state job for the company: a contract to pave U.S. Route 40. At one point, Jim took leave of absence from the company to pan for his own gold in the asphalt world, but the vein he was working played out, so he returned—to our benefit. In one of our more successful seasons, we awarded Jim with a substantial bonus and let him take a company car (a Cadillac) and a credit card for gas and motel expenses. Jim was very appreciative. In his words he felt "like a real high roller driving that Cadillac" when he took his family for ten days to Florida.

The highway 40 job was not large in the sense of length. It started at McKnight Road, in Ladue, and proceeded east to Hanley Road at the eastern edge of Brentwood. But for our opening act we could not have had a better place to introduce our big blue H. U.S. Route 40 was the western continuation across the Mississippi River of the national highway; an artery right through the very heart of St. Louis County. There was something like 78 million cars with 16 million trucks and buses registered in the U.S, and I thought they must have all been coming through Route 40. The county seat was just north in Clayton. Harrawood Brothers Inc. was a blossoming flower for all to notice. Now the eyes of unionist, machinery salesmen, government inspectors, and our competitors were all upon us. Gayle, Ed, and I took a great measure of pride in our debut.

Back Words

CHAPTER ELEVEN

Snow and Men

In our new business there was no retreat from work just because the asphalt season gave way to the winter months. We were busy with painting fonts, never-ending maintenance, and the restoration of our equipment. Then there was the snow.

Snow removal for the Harrawood Brothers became an essential part of our business in the second year. At first, we started working as individuals for Bridges, pushing snow off the Chrysler factory parking lots. However, this only lasted a couple of years because we readily took advantage of this opportunity from Jack Frost. Whenever we invested in any new trucks or machinery, we imagined how it also could work for snow removal, such as attaching a snow plow on the front. But in the first year of our snow removal business, we simply used a couple of old road-graders that we purchased. These graders had no cabs, which gave real meaning to the saying "chilled to the bone." We bought sand and salt, and broadcasted it on our clients' drives and parking lots. After a good snow year we would turn our profits into salt spreaders that fit in the beds of our trucks. We would market our business during asphalt-paving season, always reminding our customers that we were available for snow removal. By the time Harrawood Gold with the big blue H came on the scene, the company had built up a sizable clientele and equipment for snow removal.

At this point the company was well established, which led us to several other jobs, such as a significant opportunity in St. Louis County where the county basically turned over the entire Bonhomme Township to us. At one point the snow operation demanded so many resources that we had to invest in more equipment. Each year we increased our snow removal service with the county, including snow removal of large shopping centers, such as the Jamestown and Chesterfield malls. Then three years into our enterprise, we lassoed the most significant cash cow for Harrawood Brothers: snow removal for St. Louis Lambert International Airport.

In 1925 Albert Bond Lambert, a renowned Olympic medalist golfer, the president of a pharmaceutical company, and the first St. Louisan to have a pilot's license, purchased the former Lambert-St. Louis Flying Field, which was named in his honor. Lambert enhanced the field by putting in hangers, as well as passenger and mail service from which Charles Lindbergh first began flying. A few years later Lambert sold it to the city of St. Louis, and it became the first municipally owned airport in the U.S. It was also the first in air traffic control to use semaphore flags to communicate with pilots, and the first jet-age designed terminal, which inspired the terminal design for JFK International and LAX airports. In 1967 Lambert airport also advertised its first bid for private companies to remove snow from its field. We saw no reason that our company could not try to take this into our operation and we decided to prepare a bid.

According to the bid, we did not possess enough equipment to meet the qualifications so we formed up with like-minded companies that were too small to win the bid alone. We placed our bid and won. Harrawood Brothers would take the role of supervising the project. The second year we were undercut by one of our "partners," but they filed for bankruptcy, and our company took over the contract. By the following year we created a sole company for snow removal. We meticulously and legally separated our company from Harrawood Brothers and called our snow removal company the very clever name of "Snow Removal." The Harrawood Company acquired a three-year contract whereby we kept buying used equipment and placing it with Snow Removal only. Later, through hard-earned rapport with the airport officials, I was able to show the need for a five-year contract. For the most part it was left to me to lay out the basic requirements to push snow at the airport.

Back then, airport security was mostly run-of-the-mill (roll your fingers in ink)—no background investigations were required; no security briefings were given. My "yeoman" John Shunk did my reading and writing for any specifics from the airport officials. John stood at the gate, checking the list of those employees coming in and handing out badges given to us from airport security operations. About all we were told in the early years was that if we saw baggage or packages fall from the scurrying terminal vehicles we were not supposed to stop and pick them up.

Our office was a small trailer. We would fire up salamander heaters to keep warm as we worked on our equipment, and we would park our pickup trucks out front to block the raw, mind-numbing wind that swept across the tarmac. From the start I supervised the field operations, which included two dozen employees but eventually grew to about 300 on the call list. I patrolled all over the terminal, directing the operation and assigning men their tasks.

The Director of Airport Operations was Colonel Griggs. We developed a mutual respect for each other, and we became good friends. Both of us maintained a spit-and-shine approach to business, which was embedded from our military experience.

I knew other county and city personnel at the airfield from past jobs. And even though sometimes they could be difficult, I presented myself pleasantly and with good humor. I knew that politicians and bureaucrats would always be around, and, sure enough, here they were at the airfield. My cordiality with them paid dividends.

The first few years at Lambert, we plowed the snow into a windrow, which meant a loader would pick up the accumulated snow and dump it to the side. This was done to the director's specifications, but the Federal Aviation Administration (FAA) stipulations required that snow piles anywhere on the terminal were a plane hazard. This regulation required us to bring in more loaders and dump trucks and increase our manpower. The airport created a dumping area outside the terminal and this coincidentally was the only place that a steel-cleated track machine was used, a bulldozer to push away the snow now being dumped by the trucks.

Though we already had women and black Americans pushing snow, the company had to meet a compulsory twenty-five percent quota with minorities. We satisfied this by subcontracting Chester Davidson, a black businessman, who already had dump trucks but leased even more for the snow removal. Chester and I came from similar hard-scrabbled backgrounds, and over the years we became very dear and close friends. The snow operations helped us both economically stave off the wolves during the construction off-season.

A normal snowfall day in St. Louis normally generates less than an inch of snow. Big snows in December can produce five to ten inches, but this typically happens on average every five years. Blizzards that produce ten inches or more are rare and usually happen in March about every ten years. Yet I encountered three of the top ten snowfalls for Missouri in March during the years that I supervised operations: 7.3 inches in 1974; and 10 inches each in 1989 and 2008. March snows were important for the company because they came right before construction season, which filled our coffers immensely.

St. Louis can also have tremendous snow storms that lock down the entire region. I was hit with tremendous snowfalls: 12 inches on December 19, 1973; 10 more inches eleven days later on December 30; 10.9 inches on January 16, 1978; and 13.9 inches on January 30, 1982. We made money, but the operational cost was high as well.

In the first years, Snow Removal employees would leave the field for their meals, which meant they might be gone for more than an hour (sometimes hours). We decided that we needed to keep the employees at the job site, so we came up with the idea of using food vans to carry box lunches out to the men. I explained my needs to the Colonel, and our conversation led to the assignment of a hangar and office buildings of our own. Now we had an area where we could park the equipment and stay warm when we worked on downed equipment. We even set up a kitchen that supported a mess hall, and eventually provided heated trailers outfitted with bunk beds instead of paying men to stay at motels around the airfield. I was able to maintain a twenty-four-hour force for snow removal. Airport management was satisfied. Furthermore, this became a required element in the contract, which (not unexpectedly) helped assure our win for the next five-year bid.

Snow is an unpredictable business. A one-inch snow today may not be anything like a one-inch snow tomorrow. Some snows are powdery, while others are wet and heavy. Some snows are made harder by the winds that increase drifting. And then there are snows that happen at thirty-two degrees Fahrenheit versus zero degrees Fahrenheit. The colder the snow, the harder it is on men and machinery. But the best snows were the ones that didn't come. The airport took no chances; when there were snow threats on the edge of radar, I was always requested to have men stationed and ready to go. We got paid the same, weather the snow came or not. This was how it went with our snow removal business, and with each passing year, we accumulated more equipment, more expertise, and more responsibility.

Eventually, security became an ever-increasing responsibility for the airport industry, not just for Lambert-St. Louis. It started on December 21, 1988, in the skies over Lockerbie, Scotland. Pan Am Flight 103 was blown out of the sky by a terrorist bomb that a passenger brought on as checked baggage. The days of guards recognizing any of my foremen (or, for that matter, me) and waving us through the gates ended. From then on there were continuous security briefings, training for the men, and new electronic passes. Every year there were more and more world events that tightened airport security. Thirteen years after Pam Am Flight 103, the dark and incredible World Trade Center attacks occurred. This sparked even greater security, including mandatory background investigations on employees and required security training that everyone had to attend. In fact, I could have taught the classes myself since I attended thirteen of them. We always stressed to our crew and anyone sub-contracting for us not to come in if they had any outstanding warrants—even so much as an overdue parking ticket—because these instantly raised red flags. Several times I saw men being hauled away in handcuffs.

We were investing a lot of our time and resources in the airport, and maybe it was the sound of planes or the smell of the jet fuel but following in the fading footsteps of my father and Uncle Everett, I attempted to acquire my pilot's license using my GI bill.

I was lucky to find a flight instructor by the name of Brother Jerome. Brother Jerome is a Christian Brother who had a passion for teaching at Christian Brothers College, a military high school. He also taught flying lessons in his spare time. He was a patient teacher, and we got along well.

Brother Jerome worked tirelessly, preparing me for the written pi-

Chapter 11 - Snow and Men

lot's test. The night of the test, I went up to the old TWA tower at Lambert Field, which is where the FAA offices were located at that time. (For reasons I can't remember, I was there at midnight.) They had just switched the watch to a new man on duty, and he would administer the test. It was just he and I in the office. The test was supposed to take two and a half hours, but since we were both young and he had also been in the service, we started talking. I told him about my reading problem and the difficulties I had experienced. We talked and worked on the test for nearly five hours. When I finished, he graded my exam and gave me a 70, a passing score. He helped me take the test, similar to when someone helped me back in the Navy.

As far as flying goes, the aircraft seemed like another piece of heavy equipment to me, like a boat or a tractor or a dozer—with the exception of a few obvious differences. If you get lost or run out of gas, you can't just stop by a filling station for help. But that's exactly what happened to me on my first cross-country student solo flight.

I had a plan to fly from St. Louis and land in Washington, Indiana. On the way, I thought I would fly over Petersburg, Indiana, to see what the strip mines looked like. Petersburg had great big strip mines and great big heavy equipment. It was a beautiful cloudless day, so I planned a slow circle around the pits, enjoying a view of the mines. Somehow I ended up crossing the Ohio River. I decided it was time to continue my flight to Washington, but suddenly I realized I was lost. In my trusty Cessna 152 trainer, with wadded up maps in my lap, I tried hard to determine where I was. I tried to read my map and my instruments, but I was completely lost. I contacted the Federal aviation controller: "Cessna 1234, Cessna 1234 flight station? over."

"Cessna 1234 this is flight service station," the controller responded.

"Yeah, I think I'm lost."

"Do you have any idea where you MIGHT be?" he asked.

"No," I said, "I'm really lost."

He and his team had me fly in a triangular pattern so they could pick up my plane on their radar. But as I began flying in a triangle, I lost contact with them. About thirty minutes later they came back up and said, "Cessna 1234 are you still lost?"

"Yes sir, I'm still lost."

"Do you see anything on the ground, any landmarks on the ground?" the controller asked.

I looked out the window and said, "Yes, there's a railroad track going through a small town."

"All small towns have railroad tracks going through them," he said.

I looked harder and reported back that there was a water tower and that I would buzz it to see if there were any markings on it. I buzzed the tower and said, "I can see the water tower. Would the class of '69 help you any?"

Long pause. "Do you see anything else?" he asked. I looked ahead and told him I saw three radio towers sticking up out of the ground.

"We know where you are so circle the radio towers, and we'll send another plane to get you." he said. "What is the status of your fuel?"

"One tank is empty and the other tank is at one-fourth, and bobbing," I said. "I see some new construction on the highway. Should I land on that?"

He told me not to do that but to stay in the air as long as possible. Pretty soon another airplane came waving his wings indicating that I should follow him.

Then I heard on the radio, "All planes stay clear of the Bowling Green airport—we have an emergency!"

Chapter 11 - Snow and Men

Bowling Green? Am I in Bowling, Green Missouri? How could I have done that? Or was it Bowling Green, Indiana? I couldn't figure out where in the hell I was.

I followed the search plane, and as he approached the runway I followed right behind him. I thought, "Oh my God, buddy, don't stop. I've got to come in there, too." To my relief, he did a 'touch and go' and flew on. The flight service station came on the radio and told me to bring my log book in "so we could talk." I was thinking to myself that this was the end of my flying career for sure. In my debrief, the controller told me I was in Bowling Green, Kentucky, and wanted to know how I got lost. I told him that I was just not paying attention. I was surprised that he let it go. Then he asked me if I was going home that night. He advised me that I had three hours of flight time and only two hours of daylight and that he knew I wasn't qualified for night flight. He had a navigation book there so I bought it, took it to my motel room, and studied it. I studied all night the best I could but only understood a word here and there.

The next morning I got in the plane, set my compasses, got permission to take off, and left. On my way back to St. Louis, darned if I didn't get lost again. I decided to use keep flying, knowing that I needed to head west. Eventually, I came upon a huge body of water, and I remember thinking that I couldn't possibly be at the ocean yet. It turned out to be Lake Carlyle, so I knew that I should take a left and head toward St. Louis. But there was a problem: I was just about out of gas.

I was searching the terrain and saw an old yellow Piper Cub parked by a barn, so I landed in the field closest to the plane and pulled up to a house. A man came out of the house and questioned me, and I told him I needed gas.

He said, "Well this isn't a gas station but we'll take this five-gallon can up to the Shell station and get some. That will get you to St. Louis."

I asked him if there was enough octane in the gas, and he told me that it might sputter a little bit but it would get me there. He picked up the can and saw that it already contained about four gallons in it, so we poured it in the tank and skipped the trip to the gas station. I jumped back in my plane, adjusted my seat belt, and as I was hanging out the door, said good bye.

"Did you forget something?" he asked. "You forgot to pay for that gas."

So I paid for the gas and took off. There was mud on the wheels that had accumulated from my landing in the field, which I think weighed the plane down and made the takeoff a little longer than it should have been. I held my breath as the stall alarm buzzed, and I just barely cleared the trees.

I told the Lord that if I ever get out of this mess I'd never fly again. Thankfully, the rest of the trip back to St. Louis was uneventful. And I didn't keep my promise to the Lord because I did fly again. I still believe to this day that the best thing a student pilot can do is to get lost (if he don't kill himself doing it, of course). I learned more from being wrong than I did from being right, and I never got lost again. I went on to get my multiengine license, which didn't require a written test, but eventually my GI bill ran out so I pretty much stayed on the ground and focused on my business.

Our company benefited from the men who came over from Bridges Paving to work for us. Jim Spegal was one of those employees, and another was a man who became our chief mechanic and all-around fix-it guy. Dick Drew was a performer extraordinaire when it came to a torch, welding rod, or wrench. If needed, he could weld chewing gum foil—that's how talented he was. Dick just darn well looked the part, too. He was tall with straight posture and squared shoulders that complemented his face, which was weathered from years of being on the road. His heavy hands and long fingers made him deft as any artist when handling tools. For a short time while I was at Bridges, Dick was my foreman. I was greatly pleased that he was now on our team. Another man from Bridges was our brother Jim.

Jim was as experienced as we were in manual labor and the operation of heavy equipment in the construction arena. In the early years, Jim worked as our small jobs man. He was assigned a laborer, Precious Jackson, and the two of them worked together touching up odds and ends or taking the pothole tasks. Jim complemented the company, and even though he was not in the partnership, he took great pride in the overall effort. Over the years, Jim was a very productive asset as a foreman or a lead man for the Harrawood Brothers' endeavor.

After Bridges closed down, Frank took a job for an international company. He and Mom moved to Puerto Rico where he supervised at an asphalt plant. After he returned from that experience we hired him on as a foreman and later as superintendent on bigger jobs. Frank performed well when sober, and we valued his understanding of the road construction business. In fact, we wanted him along when we went to Jefferson City, the Missouri capitol, where state bids were opened and read at the Governor's Inn. However, Frank would drink in the evenings and spill 'company secrets,' which damaged our ability to effectively negotiate with others on bids. Finally, we had to leave him behind. It hurt his feelings, but the devil in the bottle just wouldn't leave him alone, and we couldn't have any more slip of the lips, sinking our ships.

One day, Frank and I were shooting grade on a parking lot job when he asked me to take the idiot end, meaning the grade rod. Frank turned his aluminum hard hat around so the brim wouldn't impede his view through the transit. When he did, I took the rod and stepped in behind him. I shadowed his moves from behind. He didn't know that I was right behind him. Frank looked through the transit to the right, looked up and over it, scratching his head. Then he looked through the transit to the left and then looked up over it. I heard him say to himself, "Where the hell did that idiot go now?"

That's when I peeked over his shoulder and yelled, "Boo!"

Frank went ballistic. "You idiot, we got work to do," he said. Though I was the owner of the company and Frank's boss, he was still the old man.

Another case in point: Frank's aluminum hard hat was his signature. It said he was an old-style road man. But he was notorious for throwing his hard hat down and kicking it when his famous temper erupted. I found a hubcap once along the road edge, and when the time was right I picked it up and mocked him by throwing it down and kicking it off to the side of the road. Frank didn't even hesitate in delivering a Grandma Elsie-style round house punch to the side of my head, causing me to fall out in front of oncoming traffic, which created a chain reaction of squealing car brakes. Some things never change.

Every payday, Frank would look over his paycheck stub and say, "I'll never live to collect my social security." One Friday at quitting time, Frank said, "Well boys, you won't be seeing me around much anymore." Frank died the next night, just two days before he was to collect his first social security check, on the following Tuesday. We all agreed that Frank died before his retirement just so he would prove himself right.

Ed and I had great respect for those who served in the armed forces. In fact, ninety percent of our employees served in the military. We supported paratroopers, divers, gunship crewmen, door gunners, and a mix of Marines, Airmen, Soldiers, and Sailors. These men were a loyal, hardworking, and well-disciplined bunch who learned from their military days how to work as a team. The men we hired ranged from WWII veterans to returning Vietnam vets. For instance, there was Bob Jones, a WWII paratrooper, who made a less than gentle glider landing beyond the beaches of Normandy. And Earl "the Pearl" Hall, who was in the army in Germany with Elvis Presley and who said Elvis was just like the regular guys, even buying Earl a beer once.

Big Al, one of our earliest employees, was a Vietnam gunship door gunner who, when he returned from "Nam," went into the restroom at the airport, took off his uniform, tossed it in the trash can, and never looked back. Not that Big Al was bitter; he wasn't. It's just that he "done did that," and it was time to move on. One day, Big Al was pushing snow at the airport when he contacted me on the radio and reported, "Tom, you have a high lift broken down over here by the National Guard."

I had several high lifts working in that region. I asked, "Which one Big Al?"

There was a moment of silence, and then Big Al's voice broke over the radio, "The Missouri National Guard."

Two of my lead men—a Marine named Roger Wakefield and one of my best supervisors, Buzz Hoffsetter, who was wounded as a gunship door gunner—were both hard-working and good men back from Vietnam.

There was Gary Evans who served in Vietnam as a Long Range Recon Patrol (LRRP) operator with the 75th Ranger Regiment. Gary stood six foot two inches, with brown hair that turned dusty blonde in the summer months, gunslinger blue eyes, and the chiseled face of a Hollywood cowboy. In fact, he really was a cowboy who worked the big spreads of Wyoming, such as Matador Ranch and Big Creek Ranch. Once, we had a widening job on Telegraph Road in St. Louis County, and Gary was standing in as a flagman, holding a long-handled STOP/SLOW sign. Gary found a fresh roadkill squirrel, so he took some twine, made a loop around the critter's neck, and while he was holding back traffic, made the squirrel dance at his feet by dangling the twine. Gary would toss the twine over his shoulder and pull the critter up his back and come to a rest on his shoulder. Kids in a school bus passing at a snail's pace shouted out the window, "What's the squirrel's name?" and "What kind of squirrel is he?" Gary said his name was Fuzzy and that he was a flying squirrel, as he twirled the squirrel around his head.

Eventually, other family members joined our company, including both of my Uncle Everett's boys: Gary Harrawood, a Vietnam vet and Navy SEAL; and Steve Harrawood, a Navy Seabee. Steve was with the first group of Navy Seabee men who built the Diego Garcia airfield in the Indian Ocean.

Then there was "smiling" Bill Stevens, a Vietnam vet who became a great friend; indeed, my very dearest friend. In September 1968, at a place called An Khe, Bill was a passenger in an overloaded cargo helicopter that crashed while attempting a running takeoff. Bill lost both of his legs from the knees down, a collapsed lung, crushed ribs, and his back was fractured in three places. He had to be revived twice when his heart stopped beating. I believe he had a heart that was too big to give up. Bill returned from Vietnam to his wife and raised a son and daughter.

I hired Bill to push snow. He always came to work wearing tennis shoes while everyone else wore buckled rubber overshoes. Everybody liked him and always showed concern when asking him whether his feet get cold. Bill would always just laugh loudly and say something funny.

I received a call from the control tower and was informed that, "there's a grader here that's hung up on a snow bank and a man is down there trying to dig it out with a cane!" the caller said. Bill worked harder than many men with legs they were born with.

Another worker, Billy Nance, was hired in the nascent years of the company. Billy suffered from *ranidaphobia*, which is the fear of frogs. He swears that a frog bit him while he was wading in a creek. He shouldn't have revealed that to us. Often frogs were tossed his way, and many times he found a frog in his thermos bottle or, when opening his lunch box, a frog would hop out accompanied by Billy's screams. Billy and I had a game we played, which was to get into each other's lunch box and take a bite out of a sandwich without being caught. One day, Billy was on a roller, watching the outside edge of the road, when I sneaked up and managed to get into his lunch box and take a bite out of his sandwich. At lunch hour I stood away and watched him discover his damaged sandwich. "Damnit, I've been guarding this all day," he said. "How in the hell did you get into my lunch?"

One of the best grader operators I've had the pleasure of knowing was Martin Pinson. In fact, when my Uncle Everett came over from Indiana and I gave him a company tour, one of the stops I particularly wanted him to see—and knew that he would appreciate—was watching Martin cut grade. Everett was impressed but noticed that Marty smoked a pipe. Everett said that pipe smokers take too much time on the job fiddling around with their pipes and that he would never hire a pipe smoker (although Everett himself smoked a pipe). I told Martin that my Uncle Everett said that I should fire him because pipe smokers waste too much time lighting their pipes.

Marty came to work the next day without his pipe, but instead he had rolling papers and a pouch of tobacco. He would try to roll a cigarette, spilling the tobacco down over his chest and onto his lap. Then his loosely rolled cigarette would go up in flames when he struck a match to it. I told Marty to go back to smoking his pipe.

These are just a few examples that showcase how we had fun and, more importantly, that all the good men who worked for me were part of our success. As I learned in the Navy, a good ship is the profit of a good Captain. I was part of the crew and was always there in the trenches with the men. I think that if you asked any of the men who worked with me, they would say I was as good a boss as any had worked with.

If you drove over a fresh laid asphalt highway during the mid to late 1970s, in any of the Missouri counties of St. Louis, St. Charles, St. Francois, St. Genevieve, Lincoln, Pike, Warren, Gasconade, Crawford, Washington, or Madison, it was likely that Harrawood Brothers Inc. had paved it. We were everywhere, laying culverts and sewer lines and making street improvements, even putting in river docks for the state.

Our company put down asphalt by the hundreds of thousands of tons. Because of the asphalt burden, Harrawood Brothers bought a Barber Greene 101 asphalt plant, capable of dropping five tons each batch. We borrowed $250,000 from the bank at 7% interest. We paid out another twenty grand for a large loader to move the materials at the plant. Our plant was located just outside of Troy, Missouri, at a local stone quarry where we purchased our aggregates to make asphalt. At the plant and on the road I had to satisfy the state inspectors. I built a great relationship with Missouri State Inspectors and, by absolute necessity, I was an ardent student of inspection tests. Some of my studies were compaction and moisture tests, rock and dirt, asphalt compaction and core tests, and asphalt temperature ranges. Personnel of the State of Missouri Department of Transportation (MoDOT) and I were on a first name basis. Many of these inspectors were flexible on variables in the road paving or widening process. And then there were those who held that no leeway or tolerance should be given. They gave no quarter when it came to the state specs. However, I still maintained a good-humored disposition with these bureaucrats. After all, I worked for their boss: Missouri taxpayers. In fact, I developed long-term friendships with most of them. I have memories of working long hot summer hours with State inspectors, and there are many stories to tell. To be sure there were some notable characters.

"Jumping Joe" (as the men and I addressed him amongst ourselves) was a pudgy man with a ruddy complexion, bulbous nose, and smattering of dark freckles that gave him a clownish look. But what really made us smile were his very round-shaped ears that were accented with fat lobes.

It was only a short minute after meeting Jumping Joe that he would start telling a cockamamie story about himself. "Have you ever wondered why I slump forward when I sit or stand?" he once asked. "Well that's because I was a paratrooper. I made so many jumps that I was always sitting like that on the planes."

The one story that finally changed his moniker from Jumping Joe to Nitro Joe was when he produced a capsule from his pocket during a lull while he waited for trucks to arrive. He said, "See this capsule?" He displayed it to the crew. "I've got a bad heart, and this is a nitroglycerin capsule. So if I should pass out, take this and place it in my mouth, and then run like hell because there's going to be a big explosion." Paratrooper-Jumping-Nitro Joe worked a good many jobs with us, and even though he could always top whatever story was being told with his own bull, he was one of the good guys.

There were days on the job when the most vital piece of machinery would break at the most crucial point. Trucks laden with material would get backed up, leaving men to sit idle and stalling an entire job. But these occurrences were just part of the job, and my men and I would jump into action, executing damage control. Despite the heat from the sun, road, and machinery mixed with the sweat and grease dripping from our arms and off our foreheads, we would manage to get the job moving again.

Our safety record was first rate when compared to other industries. There were the occasional smashed fingers, twisted ankles, cracked ribs or broken arms, but, never (thank goodness) a fatality. One occurrence that happened on McDonnell Road, next to the airport, involved my cousin, Gary. He was operating a rubber tire high lift loader, crumbing out loose material alongside the road to widen it. A water hydrant was in the pathway that should have been moved by the utilities department. Gary was careful enough as he worked up to it, constantly being monitored by Roger Wakefield. "Now be careful with this hydrant," Roger said. But as soon as he said it, Gary clipped it off, causing a geyser that sent water thirty-five feet or more upward. Roger had to run hard just to keep from being drenched. What's worse, the hydrant was on a water main that supplied the Boeing Aircraft Facilities across the street. With the water pressure dropping, it somehow triggered the fire alarms at Boeing, and a whole host of personnel evacuated the building to the sounds of bells, whistles, and sirens going off everywhere. Engineers and managers in their white shirts, ties, and white hardhats assembled around the geyser that now had created a rushing river of water beside the compound. When the "white hats" shouted up to Gary to do something, he did. He moved up to the geyser and dropped the loader bucket down over the geyser causing the water to shoot—with tremendous force—horizontally, blasting the assembled managers off their feet and washing them backward. White hardhats swished away in the current like Dixie Styrofoam cups. When a police car pulled up, a Barney Fife-type policeman came swashbuckling over to the loader and flipped open his ticket pad. He walked to the rear of the loader, but seemed profoundly incensed when he couldn't find a license tag even after he encircled the machine. (Of course loaders don't have license plates.) The water utilities men showed up, replaced the hydrant, and removed pieces of it later that day.

Good guys, good times.

CHAPTER TWELVE

"Play Ball"

    In 1972, I bought a home in a pleasant new suburb development in Ellisville. What made this location so nice was that behind the house a narrow wooded ravine separated Ed's home from mine by no more than a couple hundred yards. There was a well-worn path that connected our homes, and our kids played in this area. Our homes were modest, and other than Ed's swimming pool, we did not live or display a lifestyle beyond our means. I worked many long hours, but I made time to engage with my family.

    My interest in the fast-growing popularity of slow pitch softball that my brother Ed enjoyed, did not meet his passion for the sport. At the time, I was more of a handball player. When my brother asked me if I wanted to play on his team, I turned him down. It was only a few days later that I reconsidered, and I accepted his offer. But it was too late because Ed claimed his roster was filled.

    Competition, a fervent motivator, always existed between Ed and me. When he said I could not sign on to his team I decided right then and there to raise my own team. "I'll just get a team and beat yours," I boasted to Ed. He scoffed at my competitive threat, not because he didn't think I could raise a team, but because the slots were full, he said, due to the lack of softball fields to play on; in other words, Ed's league had them all booked up.

I did not accept Ed's premise that there were no fields to be had. But sure enough, when I searched the immediate and extended area, I was surprised to find that Ed was right. The more I looked into it the more I realized that there was a real need for ball fields. Most fields were booked up every day into the late evening hours. Could there be an opportunity here for the Brothers? The more I investigated various ball fields, the more I realized the swelling need for field time. And there were no private ball fields; the fields were all controlled by municipalities or school districts. A place to have tournaments and round robin playoffs in a concentrated area simply did not exist.

The next obvious step was for the Harrawood Brothers to come up with a plan to open a ball field. We thought of different areas that could support the plan, but in the end a fifty-acre site located in Valley Park along the Meramec River became the best prospect. The site of the old Pittsburg Plate Glass factory, with no buildings, only wild tangled undergrowth, convinced me that a lucrative prospect was available. We began formulating a plan.

There were plenty of discussions on how to separate the ball field from the paving company, with plenty of legalese from lawyers, but in the end we had to put both businesses under the same umbrella of bonding. We were laying it all on the line again—with the exception of Snow Removal.

Once the property was officially ours and the clearing and excavation began, I continued my quest to understand all I could about softball fields. I got my information (right off the bat) by talking to players themselves. I simply sat down with them and asked, "If you were building a ball diamond, what would it look like?"

The answers were direct: water fountains in the dugouts; electronic scoreboards; clean and spacious restrooms; well-lighted parking spac-

Chapter 12 - "Play Ball"

es; decent concession stands, beer. Ed and Gayle were absorbed in the research just as much as I was. (Ed was the most qualified on the subject of ball fields since he played the game and was asking the same sort of questions I was.) As we mentally tabulated these conversations, we could see the development of a future "Harrawood Field."

Gayle busied himself with details of the rules and regulations of opening a ball field, including permits and insurance to cover liabilities. Most importantly, Gayle was casting a net for the people who best understood the game of softball—those who knew and understood the inside of amateur softball. That's how Gayle found Chuck Middleton from Crestwood, Missouri. Chuck was a softball enthusiast, a future inductee of the Springfield Amateur Softball Association (ASA) Hall of Fame, a Missouri Softball Hall of Fame inductee, and a life member of the Sportsplex Operators & Developers Association (SODA). Gayle couldn't have found a more qualified person to direct the game at Harrawood Field.

Chuck, Gayle, Ed, and I sat around a table and laid out a large sheet of white paper. We drew a large rectangle representing the fifty acres designated for the field, and then we made a circle inside of that. With Chuck's guidance, we designed a rough sketch of what we would do. Inside the circle, the concession stand and restrooms would be the focal point. From this circle, we sketched a quartet of ball diamonds extending peripherally outward. The remaining space provided liberal parking. With still enough space available we sketched in one more ball field separate from the central compound. And there it was right before our eyes. I looked up and into the eyes of my brothers and recognized that twinkle of approval that I'd seen so many other times—a look that said: "We can do this."

With any large-scale development there is always going to be opposition. A small faction of Valley Park locals voiced their displeasure with the announced plan and registered their complaints to the city fathers. Their concerns ranged from the increase of traffic, noise, and night lights to the levy that we were building around the perimeter of the ball field that they thought would increase the potential for flooding from the Meramec River.

On the front porch of Ben Beckett's home, the Mayor of Valley Park, I registered my concerns and discussed the opposition. Mayor Beckett was an advocate for the development of the complex who conveyed to me a simple bit of wisdom that I incorporated as part of my business philosophy from that day on. He said, "Tom, where there's bees, there's honey; and where there's cars, there's money. Don't worry; we'll get that ball field in."

Valley Park's earliest known occupants were Mississippian Indians. French and German pioneers in the mid-eighteenth century further developed the village. First known as Nasby, Sulphur Springs, and Meramec, by 1890 the town name would be changed to Valley Park. St. Louisans at the turn of the nineteenth century and into the 1920s sought it as a refuge from the sweltering summer city heat. Boarding the Missouri Pacific and the St. Louis-San Francisco rail lines, they arrived at either one of the two town depots. Valley Park sprouted river houses, "clubhouses," and quaint cottages using the coolness of the clear Meramec River as relief. As we built our field, Valley Park was a tired and worn blue-collar river town with approaching development on the horizon.

We pulled from our workforce the men and machinery needed, and what we did not have in machinery, we rented. Our employees were a talented bunch of men, and most of the construction on the infrastructure was done by them. We rotated men from road jobs as we needed them.

We assigned Roger Wakefield as our lead construction supervisor. Ed and I divided our time between road jobs and the ball field. Gayle, as always, involved himself with matters of logistics. He took care of researching what food-handling equipment was needed, type and style of bleachers, and numerous other details that were always coming at us. One of the not-so-small details was getting a beer license. However, we applied for it under my name and got it.

Chuck, who became the official manager of the ball park, was busy setting up league schedules and tournaments, and had an office located on the site. He worked feverously in developing a smooth roster of teams and leagues, and, as a true believer, was indispensable for the cause. Chuck knocked it out of the park.

By late 1975, a beautiful modern sports complex with all the amenities, including a public address system with speakers in all locations and a flag pole (of course), was nearly accomplished.

There was one last facility that we designed and built on the complex: a playground. In all of the investigation we conducted, no men folk suggested the idea. On the other hand, the female players (whose leagues were growing exponentially in the metropolitan area)—especially the moms—readily celebrated the need for a playground. To create this, we bought an old fire truck from the city of Manchester for fifty cents. We stripped it of any "kid catchers," and from a nearby concrete plant we bought various sizes of concrete pipes. Then, sanding down the rough spots and painting them, we arranged them into mazes and tunnels. Swings and slides were provided but were never as popular as the concrete pipes.

Even though there were still some finishing touches, the plan was to open the gates of Harrawood Field in April of 1976 to slow pitch softball aficionados and American bicentennial patriots.

Once we opened our ball field, it became blatantly clear to us early on that food concession was going to be a real moneymaker. It also became blatantly obvious that when the moms played, the kids came; and the kids would nickel and dime dads who watched from the bleachers.

Food sales soared when the female teams played, as opposed to the increased beer sales when men leagues played. It went something like this: "Honey, got a game tonight so I won't be home for dinner after work." Whereas when mom had a game, we provided dinner for hubby and kids.

Offers were provided for a set price that included two softballs and two umpires for each game. Harrawood Field was a success, and the proof of this was the full bleachers every night of the week.

Chuck scheduled league tournaments and round robins, which were tournaments that matched each team against every other team. We invited teams far enough away that made it ever so inconvenient for them to return home for dinner, but still close enough that no motel accommodations were needed. It was a family atmosphere at Harrawood Field. Not only did we provide a high fenced area for the kids to play in, but we provided a babysitter, our sister Lois Ann, who later would become known as "Mother Hummer."

The Great Depression, WWII, post-war economics, and the early Cold War tamped down the issue of women's rights and the movement from the 1920s. Because of the Civil Rights Act of 1964 and President LBJ's Executive order 11375, which further identified sexual discrimination where federal contracts were involved, women's rights issues were greatly enhanced. Order 11375 and the political force from the recently established National Organization for Women (NOW) was a driving force behind the Equal Rights Amendment (ERA). The wording of this ERA proposal was fought over by feminist from the '20s on. The new feminist (principally NOW) dropped the wording about advancing female equality and adopted a different approach, which was "to look without distinction at men and women" in the workforce. In 1972, the ERA won quick congressional approval, but when sent to the States it failed to be ratified.

During this time female legislatures were devising amplification of the Civil Rights Act that was, in their view, vague in wording about discrimination of female employment in universities. The feminist concern was directed toward the hiring and employment practices of these federally financed institutions. This was Title IX.

A senator from Indiana, Birch Bayh, sponsored Title IX in the Senate. The Senator hung his political hat on constitutional issues related to women's rights. He placed emphasis on equality of women athletic programs in public schools and universities. The first act President Richard Nixon signed into law on June 23, 1972, was Title IX. There were some ambiguities with the law but it opened the door for female athletic programs in schools and universities across the nation. Women-organized sports were here to stay, and proof of the shifting winds came in 1974 when Little League Baseball voted to allow girls to play. By the time we were building Harrawood Field, this kettle of feminist cultural soup had stewed to the benefit of Harrawood Brothers' taste, and it inspired our next course of action. The spirit of team sports for women during America's 200th birthday celebration had (if I may say) come a long way, baby!

The Saint Louis Hummers

The joy of entrepreneurship paying off is exhilarating. Peanuts, popcorn, crackerjacks, beer, bats, and balls were the components that provided that achievement. Success, like Mayor Beckett's bees and honey, will draw attention. Harrawood Field was honey to bees that made their first appearance as we opened our gates. The first women's professional team sport—International Women's Professional Softball League (IWPS)— began its first season of play.

George W. Jones appeared at Harrawood Field as an amateur fast-pitch coach and player but with specific expertise in women's softball. His interest in fast pitch naturally kept him up on what was going on locally as well as nationally. It became obvious in bleacher conversation with George that he recognized an opportunity in women's soft pitch. George invited himself, more or less, for an audience with us, and his primary subject was the new IWPS.

Our focus was local even though there were deliberations prior to George about potential regional and state competitions, but it was still only talk. George's revelations of IWPS looking for teams to join the league set us to discussions and really drew our attention when he dropped the name Billy Jean King. He informed us that she was a co-owner of the Connecticut Falcons and that Ms. King was the predominant voice for professional women's sports.

Of course, Billy Jean King—with twenty Wimbledon titles, including six singles titles and four mixed doubles titles—would be promoting women's sports. We knew next to nothing about the women liberation movement, but we could look out of our window and see our diamonds filled with female softball players. And we sure knew about Ms. King's nationally ballyhooed battle of the sexes where she beat the heck out of Bobby Riggs (6-4, 6-3, and 6-3) in tennis back in 1973. Our thinking was unanimous: Why not get in on the ground floor by having the first St. Louis professional women's team of any sort—a fast pitch softball team—in a ball-and-bat-crazed town!

So we brought George in and made him the manager. George and Gayle were the ones who attended to the needed groundwork: acquisition of scouts, stipends, and lodging; insurance; team uniforms, colors and name. Because of the bird themes in sports names, such as Connecticut

Chapter 12 - "Play Ball"

Falcons, Phoenix Arizona Birds, Edmonton Snowbirds, San Diego Sandpipers, and St. Louis Cardinals (baseball and football), we selected the name Hummingbirds, shortened to St. Louis Hummers, with orange and brown for the team colors.

A team ownership conference was held in St. Louis, attended by the owner of the Falcons: Joan Joyce, also an original founder of IWPS and the national standard bearer of women's softball; Billy Jean King; and Janice Blalock, a celebrity in the Ladies Professional Golf Association (LPGA). These women were the driving force and de jure behind the league, and they became the talk of the town, along with the new St. Louis Hummers. It was at this meeting that Gayle was elected to be one of the IWPS Commissioners.

The St. Louis meeting spanned a couple of days. During that time, Ms. Blalock and Ms. Joyce wanted to get in a few holes of golf and asked me if I knew of a good course. I knew of a golf course but I had no idea what specifics actually made a good or bad course, since I played golf only one other time in Tokyo, Japan, with my shipmates from the LST 1166. We broke out our clubs, and after the first two teed off, I demonstrated rather easily that I had no idea what I was doing. After twelve different attempts, half of which were in the woods and weeds, I was asked (actually more like ordered) to just drive the cart. After the second hole I was asked to quit talking. Yet, for one hole, I can say I played with two of the foremost professional athletic women in the United States.

An exhibition game was held as a charity benefit between the St. Louis Hummers and the St. Louis Cardinals Football team with such notable players as Jackie Smith (#81), Dan Dierdorf (#72), and Jim Hart (#17). Over 10,000 came to watch the game. We were told by the beer distributors that "Hummer Field" was the second-largest beer-pumping station in St. Louis, next to Busch Stadium.

All of this was the result of that competitive spat between my brother Ed and me. For as long as IWPS existed, the St. Louis Hummers at Hummer Field were an astonishing success, with: Gayle, Ed, and me as directors; George W. Jones as general manager; Bob Umfleet as field manager; and Robin, my daughter, as the batgirl.

CHAPTER THIRTEEN

From Out of the Ashes

Perhaps our perspective, gained through success in business, presented a bit of myopia, but our ventures were doing quite well. However, we did encounter economic obstacles in the early 1970s that were telltale signs of a faltering economy.

President LBJ's "guns and butter" economy spread more butter on his Vietnam War than his Great Society. This resulted in a see-saw economy; that is to say, the simultaneous appearance of recession and inflation, giving rise to a new economic term to be later immortalized as "stagflation." After his first full term as president, he resigned from politics, ushering in Richard Nixon. Nixon, who had to contend with the war while managing the economic turmoil, resorted for a short period to Keynesian tactics (the use of government spending to boost a sagging economy). This did little to combat the inflation and budget deficits that he inherited. Years earlier, after Nixon lost his bid for the 1962 California governorship, he famously told reporters they would not "have Nixon to kick around anymore." But the Arabs in the fall of 1973 kicked him and the American economy.

America supported Israel in the October 1973 Middle East War, and in reprisal, Arabs, via the Organization of Petroleum Exporting Countries (OPEC), stopped oil exports for a short while. This move would have a devastating result on the price of a barrel of oil. In six months, the price increased from three dollars to eighteen dollars a barrel. In hindsight, we should have revisiting our contracts to add an inflation clause. We didn't, and America didn't either. When the oil spigots were turned back on, we all returned to business as usual. We stubbed our toe, but didn't trip on the energy obstacle directly in our path to prosperity. The cost of energy continued on its incremental rise, ready to destroy the American economy—and our family company—in 1979.

The thirty-ninth President of the United States, Jimmy Carter, who inherited the energy crisis, now called it the "moral equivalent of war." The persistent inflation, with a combination of soaring unemployment and diminished demand in the country's economy, only darkened the atmosphere. Then came the Iranian Revolution, followed by the taking of staff and U.S. Marines who were guarding the American embassy. This created a far greater OPEC crisis.

Carter appeared before the nation and asked Americans to deal with austerity through the building of character. I heard it as "suck it up; there's nothing I can do." This prophet's speech of malaise did little to change the angry Americans in long lines at the filling stations or the incredibly high prices at the grocery store. By July of 1979, it seemed to have come almost overnight: We had a 21% interest rate.

If we were just inexperienced, or ignorant about business and commerce, it would have been understood. But we weren't. It was the whole U.S. economy suffocating from the weight of high energy costs and the unmanageable interest rate. Harrawood Brothers Inc., along with millions of others, felt the weight of Jimmy Carter's "misery index."

We had to get creative and innovate where we could to stay afloat. At the time we had asphalt leaving our Troy plant every day, including a big job on U.S. Route 61 and another on Missouri 79. On highway 79, it called for widening the road, building out the shoulders, and overall paving. Using traditional construction methods in trench widening on shoulders usually resulted in completing about a mile per day. I came up with a train of innovations that enabled us to surpass this to three miles a day. The Missouri inspectors were ecstatic, and we stood to greatly increase our profits with these innovations.

If the price of oil per barrel increased by one dollar then the cost of buying asphalt went up $.25 a ton. In one weekend it jumped $13 a barrel, and we had over 200 thousand tons of asphalt to mix. Here's the math: $13.00 x $.25 x 200 thousand tons equals $650 thousand dollars. We still had 120 thousand tons of shoulder rock to place on the highway. To cover their fuel cost increases, the truckers raised their cost by $.36 per ton to haul it to us. The geometric increase in the cost of diesel fuel, with every piece of equipment on the job requiring diesel fuel, simply meant nothing more than a catastrophe for us. On top of this there was no locked-in rate for our loan on our asphalt plant. It went from 7% to 21%. We called for a meeting at Jefferson City with MoDOT and threatened to sue to meet these exorbitant hikes if there weren't adjustment clauses placed in the contracts. The state would never establish that precedent and suggested that we would lose this suit.

For the next nine months, no matter how efficient we were, no matter how hard I worked, I knew that we were over and done as a company. We finished Missouri 79 and all the other contracts, then returned home—broke.

Our Harrawood Gold color now took on the look of quicksand. The sting of losing a business in which you wrapped every molecule of your DNA around is much more depressing than I can explain. As we watched everything disappear, we were in a state of shock. The first shutdown was our asphalt plant. The bins were emptied, the yard cleaned up, and the office cleared out. We left everything else intact, though, with the hope that something might work out later, even while we watched the loader being hauled away.

The International Women's Professional Softball league disbanded after the 1979 season. It was just as well because we suffered another loss with the liquidation of the ballpark. The Hummer's played gallantly in the last season at Hummer field. The first year the team came in second place, and the next two seasons they were in the World Series. The Hummer players had no reason to hang their heads, nor did we, as a matter of fact. In the last season it was noted that the St. Louis Hummers, along with the Connecticut Falcons, were among the top teams financially able to survive into the 1980 season.

The effort by such notables as Billy Jean King, Janice Blalock, Joan Joyce, and the Harrawood Brothers, as well as the league as a whole created a movement in women's professional team sports. Our attempt showed that there was enough interest to justify development of other professional sports leagues.

The ballpark attracted many outsiders to the possibility of living in the growing West County region, and it gave pride to the community. The Hummer Ladies were recognized in local restaurants and other businesses. The Hummers themselves were grateful for the honor of being the first women's pro team in St. Louis. Players on the team like Margie Wright, Pat Guenzler, Cindy Henderson, Vicki Schneider, and Nancy "Boomer" Nelson along with the rest of the Hummers are still celebrated in the annals of St. Louis women's softball. The ballpark itself was a winning proposition, but it was a passenger on the sinking Big Blue H.

Thankfully, the winter of 1979-80, a colder than normal winter, brought a lot of snow with it. The contract with the airport kept the Harrawoods and many of our men fed throughout that long distressing winter. That spring I took one of our remaining motor graders and did subcon-

Chapter 13 - From Out of the Ashes

tracting work to earn money.

A few years later, in between working for others and going through the process of bankruptcy, my marriage ended. There were little fissures in our relationship long before the company collapsed that became chasms too big to ever bridge. I moved in with Mom.

Soon after, the company finally went on the auction block. The auctioneer was a friend of ours who helped arrange a few equipment packages. We also had another contractor who bought a new pieces for us. Ed and I were able to hold on to some of the equipment. We watched as the Harrawood Gold equipment was sold off to the last piece.

I would like to say that I "gutted up" and headed right back into the fray, but I didn't. Instead, I just sat with my head down for a few months. Where to go?

Down But Not Out

With the folding of our company, I had no one to read to me and no one to help on bids. But after awhile I knew I had to shake it off. I had a new business card printed up under the name "Quality Paving," and put the word out that I was available for jobs. For about a year, Ed and I helped each other out on jobs here and there. From previously laying down hundreds to thousands of tons of asphalt, now I was reduced to patching potholes. But my fate took a turn when I was hired to pave a lot at a Storage Locker.

I was hired by Greg Smith, a mid-twenty-year-old graduate from Kansas University, who had degrees in engineering and industrial waste management. Greg had started out in his own business doing construction and going wherever he sensed opportunity. Immediately, he struck me as an alert, smart, and fast-on-his-feet thinker, with an aptitude to identify profitability in impending jobs. Greg's abilities in reading and understanding statistics in projects, and relating them to me, made us a complementary pair, so we began partnering on specific jobs.

We joined forces on a contract to disassemble a floor in the old abandoned General Motors plant at Union and Bircher Streets in St. Louis. This detailed the removal of forty-two acres of a wooden floor and a railroad spur. The floor consisted of individual wooden blocks, 8x4x2 inches in size. We hauled the blocks to a landfill at a cost of $16 per yard. The unknown factor here was that we ended up paying for a huge miscalculation—the air void factor. Blocks don't stack solid when dumped into containers, so we were paying a large fee to dump air.

This sent us searching for an alternative, which we found at Dundee Cement factory in Clarksville, Missouri. We learned that they were burning waste material in their kilns to make cement. We asked if they would be interested in our blocks and were advised that if we could get the blocks down to the size of our little fingernails they would do a test burn.

Immediately, Greg and I obtained an industrial-duty wood chipper and processed a few yards for the test. It worked well, and this turned the job around quickly. Instead of paying $16 per yard for disposal, we were receiving $18 per yard, selling the blocks as fuel. This began a new company: Harrawood, Son and Smith. (Later my son Chris would leave for a tour of duty in the U.S. Navy.)

For awhile, under this company, we performed general contract work that involved laying asphalt or concrete, and whatever would come our way. However, we began doing exploratory research on railroad crossties because they had the same consistency as our wooden blocks. We crushed up a tie and sent it to a Pittsburgh laboratory for an analysis of everything that might be in that cross tie. What immediately got our attention was that the British thermal unit (Btu) in a pound of crushed crossties equaled nearly that of a pound of coal. Moreover, the creosote in the tie burns out harmlessly at 1,400 degrees versus power plants that burn at approximately 2,000 degrees. By the mid-1980s the kilns of Dundee Cement were eating our General Motors' blocks and crossties—while feeding our bank account.

Then we did some more research. Railroad ties are spaced every 19.5 inches apart, according to the Railway Crosstie Association. Based on this statistic there are something like 3,250 ties per mile. This means that from 700 million to 800 million crossties are laid under the 200 thousand miles of railway. Close to 18 million ties are replaced every year. These were statistical findings that Greg researched and read to me. We were encouraged by these numbers. We were also encouraged from the discovery that the major railways were in dire need of relieving themselves of ties. There were railway machines that would cut ties in half and then pitch them over on the sides of the tracks. Increasing environmental regulations prohibited the practice of burning them. Although there was public demand for landscape ties, this scarcely made a dent in the stacked ties, which were all over railroad properties in the United States. The very factor that led to the collapse of Harrawood Brothers—energy cost—was now offering potential prosperity. Greg and I continued testing and researching methods and equipment that could help us turn ties into fuel for power plants. By 1988, this initiative brought us together to form Wood Waste Energy, Inc.

Wood Waste Energy

Inspired by our results at Dundee Cement, we sensed another rewarding opportunity. To see if our idea would pay off, we contacted Norfolk Southern Railroad, based in Roanoke, Virginia, and requested their crossties. To our delight not only did they offer us ties, they offered to deliver them to us in a train of gondolas. We wanted them in Moberly, Missouri, the location of our first attempt at shredding bulk materials.

In Moberly, the management of Consolidated Electric Company agreed to work with us on a test burn at their power plant. It was their thought that the ties would increase BTUs, while lowering the sulfur content from the coal that was mined nearby, preserving the surface mining operations and the jobs it produced. Greg and I obtained a wood shredder from Richmond, Virginia, that pulverized the ties and then dumped this material into a hammer mill that further reduced the size. This mill didn't amount to much more than a "hay buster" when it came to busting up railroad cross ties. Ties that had been embedded with metal straps to help the wood from checking played havoc on the hammers, as did tie plates, rail spikes, and other steel scrap. It was a hard, infuriating process to get twelve hundred tons of finely crushed ties on the line.

There were positives and negatives in the final test. The first positive was that the electric company paid for the detailed and expensive environmental tests required in the process of using ties. These valuable test results were then turned over to us. The second positive came a little later to us by way of Transmission Products, owned by the Stone family of Richmond, Virginia. The wood shredder technical consultant found the tenacity that Greg and I displayed noteworthy. He passed on our concept to the management of Transmission Products. Soon thereafter a meeting was arranged in downtown St. Louis where Greg and I made a presentation and offered a proposal. A few weeks after that meeting, Wood Waste and Allan Stone, a Princeton University-degreed engineer, partnered up. I was impressed with Allan's ability to visualize our concept. We become very good friends from this business relationship, an association that gave us the needed financial resources to continue our work. With Allan, we now had a silent partner who invested fifty percent while Wood Waste pressed on.

One potential problem that we needed to overcome was that the coal was blown into a cyclone furnace, and our crushed ties impeded the feeding system; they were always clogging up the system no matter what we tried. Both Consolidated Electric management and Wood Waste worked tirelessly, trying to make it work. (It was very late at night when we made the burn, but it was clear that it would not be that effective, in this type of plant, anyway). But we had the study and the test results. And we had a new partner who provided the financial catalyst. Now we could continue our search for places to test and further develop a system that would withstand the tremendous beating of crushing crossties.

Paging through trade magazines, I came to a picture that captured my attention. I showed Greg. It was called a Traveling Grate, which was an enclosed track, resembling something like a bulldozer track. It used forced air to suspend the material. We envisioned finely crushed ties being carried on the grate to the furnace, but we needed to devise a method or a device that could withstand the enormous amount of scrap iron and other materials that were always found mixed in with the ties.

Here was the scenario: We had access to an enormous supply of fuel; we had a national mind-set to conserve using sustainable energies; and we had a consumer. For the next decade Greg and I would throw everything we had—body and soul—into developing a way to crush and shred a 7"x9"x8'5" piece of wood down to something smaller than a little fingernail, so that it would burn completely without any loss of energy in the burn. We learned from the inquiries and diligent research performed by Greg, and this led us to a biomass-fuel-powered operation in New Bern, North Carolina, on the banks of the Neuse River. Weyerhaeuser Co-New

Bern, an electric power plant, was in the process of converting biomass to energy. With the Norfolk Southern railroad building a spur and sending in the ties, Wood Waste began the development of the method to convert railroad ties into fuel.

While attending a meeting with Norfolk Southern officials, I had a senior official ask, "Harrawood, are you going to single out ties for landscaping?"

Ding, ding! A bell went off in my head. Did I just hear what I think I just heard. I answered, "Well, yeah. It is okay, isn't it? I have your company's permission to do this?"

"Oh yeah, take what you want," the granting official replied.

Up until now, I thought we were to burn all the ties, but now we had another option for some of them. The railroad crosstie community is a small, tight group, and word gets out quickly. It wasn't long afterward that Wood Waste subcontracted with a company of tie pickers. These crosstie gypsies followed us wherever we were, collecting ties and sorting out the various grades (with number ones being prime for landscaping). They paid Wood Waste a certain price per tie. And, while selecting theirs, they would stack the fuel ties off to the side and even load them in gondolas for shipping to our burn sites. Wood Waste also sorted ties and sold them to various landscape contractors. Now we had a free source of material that presented a source of revenue on both ends.

The Illinois Central Railroad, among other railroad companies, heard about Wood Waste Energy and began contacting us. They directed us to a switch yard in south Chicago, Illinois, where they had thirteen miles of rail and ties to be removed. We also made a contact in Bloomington Normal, Illinois, with a contractor who would pay us for each tie and for the scrap. I only went up to make sure that the job was going according to specs. In the end, the job was very successful.

This led to more contracts. In St. Louis we were contracted by Union Pacific to remove miles of rail ties and scrap while we continued with our Bloomington Normal contractor with similar negotiations.

By the mid-1990s, if you saw gondolas loaded with used crossties being hauled on the railways, from anywhere in the mountains and valleys of Appalachia, Alleghany, the Smokey Mountains, the coastal piedmont, across the Midwest cornfields, and the north woods of Minnesota and Wisconsin, they were likely being transported to Wood Waste Energies for processing into fuel.

Our second site for receiving and processing was in Duluth, Minnesota, and ties were now eagerly being sent to us from Burlington Northern and Santa Fe Railways. Moreover, we were being paid ten cents per tie from Burlington to take the ties! In Duluth we set up on the piers alongside of Superior Paper Company to feed their boilers with our processed biomass.

Greg and I traveled day after day, living out of the back of a van that we slept in to keep our expenses down. Meeting after meeting with railroad officials, machinists, mechanical engineers, and crosstie gypsies had brought us to a point that we had a complete new method of shredding bulk materials. On July 5th, 1995, Greg and I filed for a U.S. patent for what we called a "bulk materials shredder and method."

For our third burn site, we set up in Grenada, Mississippi at a plant that actually made crossties. We sent Illinois Central ties to this plant, and we processed the ties to make fuel for boilers that pressurized green ties into treated ties—old in and new out. This plant would have my old friend, Jim Spegal, as the manager.

I sat at my St. Louis office desk while the office girl sat next to me. She was assigned to do my reading and writing but wasn't all that excited about it (and neither was I). My dyslexia continued to frustrate me and isolate me behind my desk. It gave me a reason to retire. It was time to return home anyway. I cashed in my partnership and headed west on U.S. 50, back home to my wife and our farm. On February 11, 1997, inventors Greg M. Smith and Thomas E. Harrawood were awarded U.S. Patent 5,601,239 for our invention. Years of painstaking and often heartbreaking field work led to success.

EPILOUGE

In the spring of 1984, when I was frantically scouring for work with Quality Paving and still fighting a sadness that always tried to slink into my head, I was living not far from a pauper's life, but a ray of sunshine burst through this dreariness. This light of my life was Laura, a St. Louis girl I had known for awhile. In a simple wedding, we exchanged vows in the house where we currently live. The kitchen became our makeshift chapel, decorated with wildflowers and irises that we picked from along the ditches and roadways. It was truly a unique celebration, with an assembly of family, friends, and neighbors, topped off with a pot luck dinner and a square dance. There couldn't have been a truer soul mate designed for me, and looking back now, I cannot imagine where I would have gone in my life's journey without my Laura. The days, no matter what they brought from that point forward, simply became better. For better or worse, Laura has always been there for me.

In the early years of 1990, Gayle was diagnosed with cancer. While he fought hard, at one point Gayle was going to end his ordeal. He had a bottle of pills and a 38 caliber pistol. I went to visit him for the last time. We had a good cry and said our goodbyes. It was a rough, sleepless night for me. The next morning the phone rang. And when I answered, Gayle's voice was on the other end. I asked in a sheepish sort of manner, "Gayle, where are you calling me from?" He told me he just couldn't end his own life and that while trying to muster up the courage, he fell asleep. In the end, cancer pulled the trigger for my brother Gayle.

Shortly after Gayle's demise, my dear mother passed away. Before we closed her casket, Gayle's daughter slipped the urn of his cremains in with Mom, and we were sure that Gayle would have been delighted in knowing that he beat the funeral expense. All rest together now alongside of Frank.

The March 2007 winds chased away the remnants of the Missouri winter and taking with it the spirit of my brother Ed. How else could my brother have died, but the way he did. He had a massive stroke while playing a pickup game of basketball. If anyone in my family was affected by March Madness, it was him. It is only fitting that our old Montgomery, Indiana, high school team, the Vikings, won their basketball sectional tournament the same weekend that Ed died.

My son, Chris (and my new business partner), and I reorganized Snow Removal. We owned all the equipment so we were way ahead financially. That was one of the reasons that, after four and a half decades of removing snow, both of us decided it was time to fold. In addition, no serious accident had happened during our four decades of operation, such as crashing into a jet airliner, which was always a great concern of mine. What's more, most of the airport staff that I had known from the very start were retiring or being replaced, cronyism and political correctness were increasing, and I was fighting cancer.

Over the years, Snow Removal increased from less than a dozen personnel to a snow crew of more than 150, with five full-time employees who worked at the airport and maintained the equipment. This gave seasonal economic support to our family. Nearly all the nieces and nephews, our sister, and brother, Jim, worked in the business in one facet or another. The enterprise just didn't come together magically; it took several winters to fine-tune this operation. I would be the first there and the last to leave during the whole time we managed the contract. I missed only one snow

Epilouge

when I had a surgery. Yet, in 2011, I finally closed the business, and took with me an immense store of friendships with good and lasting memories. During our time at Snow Removal, my niece, Vicky, and my son, Chris, did my reading. Chris and I would now strike out in another venture.

Now, from my Missouri home, U.S. Route 50 is the same distance as Route 50 was from our Indiana Basement House. But in Indiana I lived south of the highway; here in Missouri, I live north.

On U.S. 50, just a mile from my home, a twelve-acre parcel of land went up for sale. It was a former truck sales business. Remembering Mayor Beckett's correlation of bees to honey and cars to money, Chris and I acquired this property, which is now the site of Harrawood Equipment Company, LLC. With his business insight, Chris did extensive research and obtained dealerships for major brands of equipment that we now rent, sell, or service. Occasionally, I stop by and give a hand to Chris and the growing staff, but mostly I sit back with a great measure of delight and watch my son, read, write, and execute the daily operations of our newest enterprise.

My daughter, Robin, comes in to Harrawood Equipment twice a week to help with the business. She does a little janitorial work, and some sales and office work. It is a pleasure to watch these two rib each other, and me. Life is a book, and I value every page that's turning.

Back in 1977, during our exhibition game between the St. Louis Hummers and the St. Louis Cardinals football team, we sent out VIP invitations. On the very top of the list was our Uncle, Thomas Earl McKinney, who came down from Michigan. Uncle Earl was a great inspiration for my brothers and me. He was an enterprising man who clawed himself out of the Kentucky coal mines and migrated to Michigan where he became a very successful and competent top-level manager in the automobile manufacturing business. Uncle Earl and I were standing together looking out over the newly built Hummer field. The flag was snapping and music blared from the speakers, stirring the crowd. An intense sunset put me in a bit of a melancholy mood. When I spoke to Uncle Earl, I said "Uncle Earl, I sure wish I could read and write. It's just like being confined to a wheelchair that has a broken axle. What might I have accomplished?"

Uncle Earl studied me for a bit, then said, "Tom, let me tell you a story that I've heard about an immigrant who came to America and could not read or write. He saw a sign in the window, but didn't understand it. He asked a passerby what it said, and it was read to him, 'Help Wanted.' So the immigrant went inside and asked for the job. He was told they needed a bookkeeper for a whorehouse. He explained that he couldn't read or write. 'Well that won't do,' said the hirer, 'you must be able to read and write to be a bookkeeper in a whorehouse. But here's a quarter for your effort.' The immigrant walked outside and bought two apples for a quarter from a street vendor and, in turn, sold them for double the amount he paid. In time, he became the largest and wealthiest produce merchant in the city. One afternoon his bookkeeper asked him to read something. He told his bookkeeper he couldn't read or write. The bookkeeper recoiled and asked, 'My God, man, what would you have been if you could have been able to read and write?' The immigrant said, 'A bookkeeper in a whorehouse.'"

What Uncle Earl was telling me that evening was that we all have our place under the sun and we all have talents that we can develop—that prospect is everywhere in this great America. But while the opportunities exist, one must seize the initiative. To have success, one must know failure. I cannot read or write, but I can listen. One of the early mid-twentieth-century inventions was the television, and from a young age I could watch, listen, and learn. I learned how many things were done from tele-

Epilouge

vision shows, such as "Industry on Parade." It has been said a picture is worth a thousand words. Over the years, there were many times when I'd look at pictures of equipment and realize how I could improve them. However, these days, it is the history channels on television that captivate my attention and provide a great many lessons. For example, I recall USMC General James "Mad Dog" Mattis once said something like he never lost sleep over the possibility of failure; "I cannot even spell the word," he stated.

Perhaps in a way I am like the General and the Immigrant. I cannot fret over the negative possibilities of something not happening; I can only go with my natural instinct, which is to examine the situation and then master the task. Old Duke Ellington said something on the order of, "There's more ways to dance than with your feet." I like that.

Over the years I have tried to delve into this strange inability to decipher the mystery of the written word. I've bought beginning readers, I've listened to cassette tapes, and I have worked with school teachers, all with very little accomplishment.

One day, I knocked on the office door of a Meramec College professor and sat down in front of him. I explained my greatest desire. He said he would not enroll me into any class, but would instruct me himself. We worked together for many months. Later, he asked if I would be willing to work even more with a colleague of his, an M.D. with a PhD specializing in this type of disability. Apparently I was an excellent candidate because of my age, experience, and severity of my dyslexia. In the end, with much investigation, questioning, and observation from behind a one-way window, I went as far as I could go with conventional help. The professors informed me that, at best, I would retain a third-grade level. I was back in the Cannelburg school house in Miss Donahue's third-grade class.

This is the first book I have ever read.

www.ingramcontent.com/pod-product-compliance
Lightning Source LLC
Chambersburg PA
CBHW071317110526
44591CB00010B/927